The True Story of the Old Testament

The True Story of the Old Testament

Responding to God's Revelation and Redemption

This inductive Bible study is designed for individual, small group, or classroom use. A leader's guide with full lesson plans and the answers to the Bible study questions is available from Regular Baptist Press. Order RBP0101 online at www.regularbaptistpress.org, e-mail orders@rbpstore. org, call toll-free 1-800-727-4440, or contact your distributor.

REGULAR BAPTIST PRESS

The Doctrinal Basis of Our Curriculum

A more detailed statement with references is available upon request.

- The verbal, plenary inspiration of the Scriptures
- Only one true God
- The Trinity of the Godhead
- The Holy Spirit and His ministry
- The personality of Satan
- The Genesis account of creation
- Original sin and the fall of man
- The virgin birth of Christ
- Salvation through faith in the shed blood of Christ
- The bodily resurrection and priesthood of Christ
- Grace and the new birth
- Justification by faith
- Sanctification of the believer

- The security of the believer
- The church
- The ordinances of the local church: baptism by immersion and the Lord's Supper
- Biblical separation—ecclesiastical and personal
- Obedience to civil government
- The place of Israel
- The pretribulation rapture of the church
- The premillennial return of Christ
- The millennial reign of Christ
- Eternal glory in Heaven for the righteous
- Eternal torment in Hell for the wicked

Alex Bauman, Editor
THE TRUE STORY OF THE OLD TESTAMENT:
RESPONDING TO GOD'S REVELATION AND REDEMPTION
Adult Bible Study Book
Vol. 62, No. 3
© 2014 Regular Baptist Press
www.regularbaptistpress.org • 1-800-727-4440
Printed in U.S.A.
All rights reserved
RBP0104 • ISBN: 978-1-60776-839-5

Contents

Preface

The *True Story of the Old Testament* is an overview study of the Old Testament. It is designed to present God's dealings with humanity in terms of His self-revelation and redemptive activities. It includes a chronological examination of God's dealings with people, especially with His people Israel, as recorded in the Old Testament Scriptures. It explains how God brought the world and Israel into existence. It highlights this explanation with frequent references to God's love, mercy, and grace. This study also relates how God worked faithfully with Israel and some of the important blessings He has promised to Israel—especially as seen in His covenants with Israel. And this study distinguishes God's dealings with Israel from His dealings with the church.

As an overview, this study is better understood as a "fly over the land" type of study and not a "slow drive through the scenic route" type of study. It is important that you understand this design.

Expect to get from Genesis to Malachi in thirteen studies. That is a good thing. You will gain an invaluable and comprehensive level of knowledge that will serve as a base for future Bible study. Expect to pass by or pass over many interesting "sights" that deserve a visit the next time you are in that portion of the Bible. This, too, is a good thing. The curiosity created by noting such points of interest can serve as motivation for additional study of God's Word.

Enjoy studying *The True Story of the Old Testament*. Enjoy the quick pace and the sharp focus on the revelation of God and the redemption of mankind.

Introducing the Old Testament Story

Studying Old Testament books is valuable because they are God's revelation of Himself and His plan for redemption.

2 Timothy 3:15–17; Psalm 119

"All scripture is given by inspiration of God, and is profitable for doctrine, for reproof, for correction, for instruction in righteousness: That the man of God may be perfect, thoroughly furnished unto all good works" (2 Timothy 3:16, 17).

Asling and a stone, a lion's den, a golden calf, a whale, and a fleece. All of these objects probably triggered in your mind scenes of Old Testament accounts. Perhaps you also thought of learning about these accounts as a child.

The Old Testament is filled with narratives with all kinds of action and drama. But the Old Testament is much more than a collection of stories that are entertaining to read. The Old Testament is meant to impact our lives of faith and help us understand God. This study will help your realize the impact of the Old Testament on your life.

Getting Started

1. Why are narrative accounts impactful teaching tools?

2. How have Old Testament accounts impacted your life of faith?

Searching the Scriptures

Value of the Old Testament

The Old Testament is a valuable source of God's revelation for many reasons. The Old Testament is part of God's Word; thus it has inherent value. Many Biblical themes, doctrines, and motifs find the bulk of their support in the Old Testament. The Old Testament relates the beginnings of creation, sin, and Israel. The New Testament authors extensively quote and allude to Old Testament texts. The Old Testament contains hundreds of prophesies about Jesus Christ and the future. Yet, many Christians under appreciate this treasure trove of instruction.

3. Why might believers not value the Old Testament?

4. When was the last time you chose to read or study the Old Testament?

5. Read 2 Timothy 3:15–17. What Scriptures did Paul have primarily in mind in these verses?

6. According to these verses, what can the Old Testament accomplish in the lives of Christians?

7. How does viewing these verses as primarily referring to the Old Testament change or increase your appreciation for the value of the Old Testament?

Psalm 119, the longest "chapter" in the Bible, is a hymn extolling the worth of Scripture. Nearly every verse says something about the law of God, about His precepts, or about His ordinances.

8. Read through several sections of Psalm 119. Record ten benefits of the Old Testament Scriptures recorded in that Psalm.

9. How would you summarize Psalm 119's teaching on the Old Testament scriptures?

In the middle of Psalm 119, a paragraph exalts the practice of meditating on God's law (119:97–104). The psalmist explained how he loved God's law and how he had made it the focus of his meditation throughout the day. God's commandments impart wisdom, insight, and understanding. The psalmist rehearsed his commitment to follow God's Word and relished the sweetness of God's Word. Christians today should approach the Old Testament with the same joy and passion. The Old Testament perspective of itself is much like Paul's perspective of the Old Testament (2 Tim. 3:15–17).

Orientation to the Old Testament

This course looks at the Old Testament in its entirety and relates its major truths in terms of its continuous narrative. This overall approach recognizes the singular, divine authorship of all the Old Testament books. Different holy men of God communicated the various accounts, but God by His Spirit moved the men of the Old Testament to record His message (2 Pet. 1:21).

The story of the Old Testament, then, is God's story. God revealed Himself throughout the books. It is "His story."

Introducing the major divisions, genres, historical setting, and cultural and linguistic factors helps you appreciate the overarching story and themes found in the Old Testament. And this study will be more effective by considering them.

10. What difficulties do you anticipate in studying the Old Testament?

Major Divisions

The Old Testament is one story. But at the same time, the Old Testament is a collection of thirty-nine books with a mix of history, law, poetry, and prophecy. When we consider the variety of books, it might be helpful to think of the Old Testament books sitting on a five-shelved bookcase. Each shelf represents a major division of the Old Testament.

11. Why is an awareness of the divisions of the Old Testament an important factor in understanding particular passages?

On the top shelf of the Old Testament bookshelf are Genesis, Exodus, Leviticus, Numbers, and Deuteronomy. The shelf is labeled "The Pentateuch," which means "Five Books." Moses wrote these five books.

Genesis relates the creation of the world, the fall of humanity into sin, Noah and the Flood, the call of Abraham, and the accounts of the

Patriarchs (Abraham, Isaac, Jacob, and Joseph). Exodus explains how God delivered Israel out of Egypt and how He gave His law at Mount Sinai. Leviticus records many specific laws concerning the tabernacle and ritual purity. Numbers begins with genealogies, adds more legislation, records how Israel broke the law and how God took care of His people throughout their wilderness wanderings.

The Pentateuch is filled with examples as well as guidance. The laws in the Pentateuch are not directly applicable to Christians (Rom. 6:14). Nevertheless, the law provides insight into God's attributes.

12. Name an impactful lesson you learned from the Pentateuch.

On the second shelf are twelve history books. These books run from Joshua to Esther.

Joshua records the conquest of the Promised Land by the people of Israel. Judges records the cycle of sin, oppression, and deliverance in the chaotic days before Israel had a king. Ruth provides a precious story of belief and obedience during the days of the judges.

The books 1 and 2 Samuel explain why Saul was unfit and why David was fit to be king of Israel. The books 1 and 2 Kings explain how Israel split into the two smaller kingdoms of Israel and Judah following the reign of David's son Solomon. The books 1 and 2 Kings assess the kings in terms of their faithfulness to the Law of Moses. They record how ultimately both kingdoms were destroyed and the people were deported because of their unfaithfulness. They also describe the ministries of Elijah and Elisha. The books 1 and 2 Chronicles relate much of the same material as 1 and 2 Kings, but the Chronicler judged the kings, especially the kings of Judah, for the ways that they treated the temple, the priests, and the sacrificial system.

Ezra, Nehemiah, and Esther recount the return of some of the Jews from captivity to the Promised Land. The book of Ezra, named for a priest, emphasizes the rebuilding of the temple. The book of Nehemiah, about an administrator, emphasizes the rebuilding of the wall. Esther, named for a member of a Gentile court, emphasizes God's providential care for His people as they lived among the nations.

13. Why might knowing Israel's history be valuable for Christians?

On the third shelf are the books Job, Psalms, Proverbs, Ecclesiastes, and Song of Solomon. They are all poetic in nature.

Job, a righteous man, conversed with his friends about the age-old question, "Why do the righteous suffer?" Toward the end of the book, God Himself spoke, and Job withdrew his contention with God.

The book of Psalms includes 150 of Israel's ancient hymns, written by various people and covering various topics. The book is exceedingly rich with insightful theology and self-analysis.

The book of Proverbs provides numerous wise sayings by Solomon and others. Ecclesiastes provides a realistic perspective on humanity's ability to answer all of life's questions. The Song of Solomon is composed of vivid love poetry spoken between a woman and Solomon.

14. Which poetry book is your favorite? Why?

15. Why is poetry an effective communication method?

On the fourth shelf are the books of Isaiah, Jeremiah, Lamentations, Ezekiel, and Daniel. This shelf is labeled "major prophets." Lamentations is a poetic lament for the destruction of Jerusalem.

On the fifth shelf sit the twelve "minor prophets." These books run from Hosea through Malachi. The books contain some of the most gripping prophetic material in all of Scripture.

16. How have the fulfilled prophecies of the Old Testament strengthened your faith?

17. Describe a time when you used fulfilled prophecy in an evangelistic conversation.

We can rejoice that God has given us the Holy Spirit to help us understand Scripture (Eph. 1:17, 18). We can also increase our awareness of the distinctive characteristics of the Old Testament and be better equipped to learn from this portion of God's Word.

Different Perspectives

The practices of ancient Israel differ from those of the church. For this reason, the Old Testament can seem detached, almost otherworldly. We rightly acknowledge that we are not under the law of the Old Testament (Rom. 6:14). The tabernacle, temple, feasts, sacrificial system, and priestly order are not part of God's instructions for the church. While the practices of ancient Israel are different than our practices as believers today, we can gain a greater understanding of Jesus Christ and His redemptive work.

18. What are some correlations between the practices of ancient Israel and Jesus' redemptive work?

Diverse Literary Styles

Those who decide to read through the Old Testament may find that the diversity of the literary styles confusing. Recognizing the assortment of literary styles is essential to effective Bible interpretation.

Narratives record accounts. Every narrative has three components: plot, characters, and setting. The plot is the storyline; it reveals the relationships among the characters in the setting of their lives. While reading the accounts of the Bible, readers should look for repeated words or phrases. The repetitive phrasing makes accounts more memorable; the repetition of words or themes gives structure to longer narratives.

When observing narrative literature, we should remember some keys points. First, narratives are primarily accounts of how God dealt with mankind. We need to look for God in every account we study. His dealings with mankind will almost always translate to some degree into our lives. The ways people related to God in the accounts are meant to be examples for us.

Second, narratives have value as they are; we do not have to read symbolic meanings into them. Some Old Testament narratives, however, illustrate New Testament truth. Those narratives become symbols of spiritual truth only if the Scriptures designate them as such.

Third, narratives do not teach doctrine directly, rather they illustrate doctrine taught elsewhere. For instance, the book of Judges shows what happens when people deliberately turn their backs on Biblical truth (Judg. 2:10–23).

Fourth, we need to look at the facts as they are presented without getting sidetracked by what is not presented. God never intended for us to know what He did not reveal to us.

Fifth, we need to remember that the stories fall into different dispensations, or systems of revealed commands and promises regulating human affairs. What God expected during a past dispensation may not be what He expects today.

Biblical **poetry** helps us understand the total experience of the life of faith. It assists us in expressing our emotions to God and others, teaching us to trust and pray.

The primary characteristic of Biblical poetry is parallel structure, where two thoughts are placed in relationship to each other. This literary structure of pairing provides an immediate context in which to interpret the verse.

Observing parallelism is important. It will tell us how to interpret the phrases in poetry. But we have to be careful when the poetry uses picturesque language. We cannot take the word pictures literally. Rather, we should determine what truths the word pictures reveal.

Wisdom literature is poetry that teaches us how to live with Biblical skillfulness. It shows us how to apply truth to reality. We find wisdom literature in the startling directness of Proverbs, teaching how the naïve must make every effort to become wise. The philosophical meanderings of Ecclesiastes and the dialogues of Job with his friends are also wisdom literature.

Prophetic literature contains predictions of future events. Some of those predictions have already come to pass. The prophecies yet to be fulfilled look ahead to the day when God will cleanse and restore His creation and when Christ will rule.

Some of the prophetic literature is apocalyptic, meaning "hidden." The writer's meaning is hidden in the symbols he used. Apocalyptic literature often employs figurative or symbolic language in mind-stretching ways (see Ezek. 10; Zech. 1:7–17). These symbols go beyond the normal use of figures of speech in poetry.

When observing prophetic literature, we need to understand when the prophets ministered and to what future events their prophecies pointed. We also need to be careful not to get lost in the obscure. We should understand what we can and move on to interpretation and application.

19. Why does recognizing genre help believers understand what they are reading?

Cultural and Linguistic Differences

The Old Testament way of life seems far removed from that of modern times. For example, family members sometimes lived in separate tents (Gen. 31:33) and a widow took off her brother-in-law's sandal and spit in his face if he refused to marry her (Deut. 25:7, 9; cf. Ruth 4:7). Customs like this seem so alien to modern life that they may perplex us.

The New Testament was originally written in Greek. Both Greek and English are Indo-European languages. The Old Testament, on the other hand, was written in Hebrew and Aramaic, both Semitic languages. Therefore, English is closer to Greek than to Hebrew or Aramaic. This means that the Old Testament, even in the English translation, can sometimes be perplexing. With a little patience, however, readers of English can soon discover the pleasant way that Hebrew enables memorable storytelling.

Making It Personal

20. Why do you value a study of the Old Testament?

21. Complete the following statement: Based on the personal value that a study of the Old Testament has to me, I choose to commit to this study. I will seek to carry out this commitment by . . .

22. Memorize 2 Timothy 3:16 and 17.

Lesson 2

Revelation and Redemption at Creation

God revealed Himself as creator to His creation.

Genesis 1—3

"In the beginning God created the heaven and the earth" (Genesis 1:1).

Recognizing God as creator is essential to a worldview that is true and in touch with reality. All other worldviews could never explain life. They are essentially exercises in insanity. It is no wonder that those who refuse to recognize God as their creator clamor to get in touch with reality.

Getting Started

1. What difference does it make in people's lives to know that God created the world?

2. How does a failure to acknowledge God's role as creator impact one's view of the world?

19

Searching the Scriptures

The Old Testament story begins with God (Gen. 1:1). It assumes His existence. Without God, there would be no Old Testament story. At the beginning of the world, God had already existed. He is the eternal One, infinitely predating His creation of the world (Ps. 90:2).

3. Why does believing that Someone, God, rather than something, matter and/or energy, always existed change a person's worldview?

Genesis 1 repeatedly makes it clear that God is the only One Who participated in the creation of the world. By faith we understand that God created the matter of the universe out of nothing on the very first day of creation (Gen. 1:2; Heb. 11:3). When God first created the matter, it was "without form and void," that is, it was formless and uninhabitable (Jer. 4:23). God spent the rest of the creation week fashioning the formless and uninhabitable substance into an inhabitable universe.

4. How does the fact that no human witnessed creation impact what anyone believes about the origins of the world?

The Creation Week

The first chapter of Genesis shows the orderly way by which God fashioned the world into a place for habitation. The chapter repeats several phrases to emphasize God's orderly work of creation: "Let there be," "and there was," "that it was good," "and the evening and the morning." God's orderliness also surfaces in the activities of each of the six days.

On the first three days, God made the world ready for its inhabitants. He "divided the light from the darkness" on day one (1:4), "made the firmament" and "divided the waters" on day two (1:7), and made "dry land appear" (1:9) and "bring forth grass" on day three (1:11).

On the last three days, God created the inhabitants. On day four He created "lights in the firmament" (1:14). On day five He created "every winged fowl" and the sea creatures (1:21). On the final day, God made "the beast of the earth" (1:24, 25) and man (1:26)

The phrase "evening and morning" shows that God created the world in six literal twenty-four-hour days. Also, the Hebrew word for "day" when used with a number always refers to a twenty-four-hour day. Additional evidence appears in Exodus 20:11, since the creation week provides the basis for the regular workweek. Those who try to fit ages of time into the creation week account violate foundational rules for Bible interpretation.

5. What are some attributes of God demonstrated through His creative works?

6. How does reflecting upon God's six-days of creation affect your awe of God?

God's greatest creative work took place at the end of the sixth day of creation. On that day, God made mankind in His image and likeness (Gen. 1:26). After God had finished making everything else besides the first humans, He "saw that it was good" (1:25). After He had finished creating Adam and Eve, God saw that everything was "very good" (1:31).

Every human has worth because they are in the image of God. They should not be murdered (9:6) or cursed (James 3:9). An evolutionary model leaves man as a product of chance with no real value. So an evolutionist does not have a basis for saying murder or even hatred is wrong. Without God, any standard of right and wrong is arbitrary and relative at best.

Creationism also teaches the inherent worth of women in particular since the image of God exists in both genders, for God created mankind in His image by creating mankind "male and female" (Gen. 1:27).

7. What are some examples from history of a failure to acknowledge God as creator resulting in people devaluing humanity?

The Old Testament tells the story about God and those made in His image. Since humans are made in the image of God, they are to function as God's ruling representatives on the earth (Ps. 8:5–8). Humans are to "subdue" the earth and to "have dominion" over its animal life (Gen. 1:28) prudently rather than irresponsibly.

God rested on the seventh day because He had completed His work of creation (Gen. 2:1–3), not because He was tired. At that time, the Lord sanctified the seventh day (1:3).

8. How should you respond to the power God showed in creating the universe?

The Sixth Day of Creation

Genesis 2:4–25 enlarges our understanding of the creation of Adam and Eve recorded in 1:26–29. In Genesis 1, God seems more distant from His creative activity; He speaks, sees, makes, and blesses. In Genesis 2, God appears much closer to His creation. God formed man out of the dust of the ground and breathed into his nostrils (2:7). God fashioned the woman from a rib that He had taken out of the man and took the woman to the man (2:21, 22). In Genesis 1, God repeatedly said that His work is good, but in 2:18, He said, "It is not good that the man should be alone." In Genesis 1, God granted dominion to mankind (1:28). In Genesis 2, Adam exercised his dominion by naming the animals (2:19). Genesis 1 ends with everything being "very good." Genesis 2 ends similarly, but more subtly, with Adam and Eve "not ashamed" (2:25).

9. How do the differing focuses of Genesis 1 and 2 help you get a more complete picture of God?

10. How should you respond to the personal closeness of God as your creator?

Genesis 2 closes with an explanation of the origin and nature of marriage. God ordained marriage as the most lasting of human relationships ("shall cleave" and "one flesh"; 2:24). The man leaves his parents to marry the woman and form a new family unit. God's original place for marriage was the union of one man and one woman, but humanity soon distorted God's plan (see 4:19).

11. How does the explanation of the origin and nature of marriage strengthen or change your view on current societal distortions of these issues?

Sin Enters the World

12. What difference does it make in people's lives to know how sin entered the world?

The Lord could not have been clearer in His expectation of Adam and Eve. Adam and Eve could eat from any tree in the Garden of Eden ("every tree"; 1:29; 2:9, 16), including the tree of life (2:9), except they could not eat from the tree of the knowledge of good and evil (2:16, 17).

The Devil, or Satan, used the serpent to tempt Eve to eat from the forbidden tree. The serpent was a most clever animal in its unfallen condition (Gen. 3:1). Eve was not surprised the Devil spoke through the serpent. The serpent began with a question designed to plant doubt or to instigate a reexamination of God's expectation and warning (3:1). The serpent followed up with a lie and a distortion of the truth (3:4, 5). Eve was deceived (1 Tim. 2:14). It is true that after Adam and Eve ate the fruit, their eyes were opened (Gen. 3:7). They did become like God in knowing good and evil (3:22). However, their knowledge led to suffering and death, separation from God (3:24).

Eve succumbed to the three lines of temptation found in 1 John

2:6 and Genesis 3:6. "Good for food" was the appeal to the "lust of the flesh." "Pleasant to the eyes" was the appeal to the "lust of the eyes." And "desired to make one wise" was the appeal to the "pride of life."

13. What are current examples of temptations categorized as "lust of the flesh," "lust of the eyes," and "pride of life?"

Eve took some of the fruit and ate it. Then she gave some to her husband, and he ate it (3:6). Their eyes were opened to evil since they had just experienced it firsthand. Immediately, they were overcome with their own guilt and the shame of their nakedness since they were no longer innocent. Adam and Eve tried to sew "aprons," girdles or loincloths, to cover their nakedness (3:7). Their attempts to cover their nakedness and to hide from God among the trees of the garden (3:8) illustrate the futility of humanity in dealing with its sin problem.

14. How do people attempt to cover their sin today?

Punishment of the Guilty

God asked a series of questions to elicit a confession from Adam and Eve (3:9, 11a, 11b, 13). Adam blamed God and his wife (3:12), and Eve blamed the serpent (3:13). Of course, God saw right through the blame shifting and punished the serpent, the woman, and the man each according to his or her deed (3:14–19).

15. Why do you think blame shifting is such a common response to confrontation?

The serpent would go about on its belly and would be completely humiliated (3:14). The hostility between women and snakes serves to illustrate the hostility between God and Satan (3:15). The woman was cursed with pain in childbirth and given a subordinate role to her husband (3:16). The man was cursed with a life of hard toil as he worked the soil and fought the weeds (3:17, 18). His life would end in death and a return of his body to the soil from which he had been taken and with which he had toiled (3:19).

16. What is the most adverse effect of sin on your life?

Provision of Grace

On the darkest day of human history, we see the brightness of God's grace. God promised that the woman would give birth, though in pain, and that the human race would continue (3:16). God promised that the man would have food to eat, although he would fight the weeds to get it (3:18, 19). God made clothing of animal skins—superior to the clothing Adam and Eve had made out of fig leaves (compare 3:21 with 3:7). God protected Adam and Eve from the tree of life to prevent them from living forever in sin and in separation from Him (3:22, 23).

The most noteworthy grace promise appears in 3:15 (cf. Rom. 16:20). God promised that the seed of the serpent (Satan) would harm ("bruise his heel" at the crucifixion) the seed of the woman (Jesus) but that the seed of the woman would deal a mortal blow ("bruise thy head") to the seed of the serpent.

Genesis 3:15 provides the earliest indication of God's redemptive work. The human race sinned in Adam, so death spread throughout the entire race (Rom. 5:12). Conversely, just as many are sinners in Adam, so also many are declared righteous in Jesus Christ (Rom. 5:18, 19). Everyone who by faith accepts the substitutionary death of Jesus Christ is made righteous. Although Jesus suffered at His crucifixion ("bruise his heal" in Gen. 3:15), He rose victorious from the grave and offers salvation to anyone who believes in Him. In this way, Jesus has triumphed over Satan by rescuing sinners from Satan's dominion.

17. How should we respond to God as our redeemer?

From the very beginning, the Old Testament story shows the major themes of the revelation of God and the redemption of mankind. The remainder of the Old Testament, as well as the whole of the New Testament, explains how God has worked to extend to all humanity the fellowship He had enjoyed with Adam and Eve.

Making It Personal

18. God's creative works and interaction with Adam and Eve demonstrate several of His divine attributes. Record five attributes you learn about God from the creation week.

19. What will you do today to praise God for these wonderful truths?

Genesis 1—3 present God as the authoritative creator of the universe and humans in particular. He sets the parameters and agenda for our lives.

20. How does God's identity as the authoritative creator manifest itself in your life?

21. What will you do this week to heighten your appreciation for and submission to God's authority?

22. Memorize Genesis 1:1.

Revelation and Redemption after the Fall

God punishes sin yet shows He is merciful.

Genesis 4—9; 11

"And God saw that the wickedness of man was great in the earth, and that every imagination of the thoughts of his heart was only evil continually. . . . But Noah found grace in the eyes of the LORD" (Genesis 6:5, 8).

H e's strict!" Young people often use that short description to describe a teacher or parent who enforces the rules without much mercy or grace. Sometimes they describe more laid back teachers as "nice," "easy," or "good." Of course, a balance between the two is ideal.

Getting Started

1. Would you prefer a strict teacher or a laid back teacher? Why?

2. Would you describe God as strict or laid back? Explain.

God strikes the perfect balance between judgment and mercy and grace. He dealt with Adam and Eve with that perfect balance.

3. Read Genesis 3:22–24. How was Adam and Eve's banishment from the Garden of Eden both an act of judgment and mercy by God?

4. Do you consider death as a merciful act? Why?

After their expulsion from the Garden, Adam and Eve had two sons, Cain and Abel.

Cain Kills Abel

Cain was a farmer. Abel was a shepherd (Gen. 4:2). Accordingly, Cain brought an offering to the Lord from the fruit of the ground while Abel brought some of the firstlings of his flock. The Lord "had respect" for Abel and his offering because he offered it in faith. Abel obtained a testimony "that he was righteous" (Heb. 11:4). But God did not have "respect" for Cain and his sacrifice (Gen. 4:4, 5).

Cain became very angry because the Lord did not regard his sacrifice. Even his facial expression became contorted (Gen. 4:5). Cain's anger is not surprising given his state of unbelief. When he offered his sacrifice, he was unrepentant.

God then promised Cain that He would accept him if he offered his sacrifice in faith. God also warned Cain that if he did not do the right thing, sin would be crouching ("lieth at the door") or desiring to have Cain. Cain was faced with a choice: He could allow sin to pounce on him, or he could "rule" over it (4:7).

5. Do you typically consider warnings to be merciful statements? Explain?

6. How was God's warning to Cain an act of mercy?

When Cain and Abel were in a field, "Cain rose up against Abel his brother, and slew him" (4:8). The text emphasizes again the fact that Cain killed "his brother." So Cain murdered his righteous brother.

7. Read 1 John 3:12. Why did Cain kill his brother?

The Lord asked Cain about his brother's whereabouts to elicit a response of repentance (Gen. 4:9). Cain responded, instead, with a lie ("I know not") and coldhearted apathy ("Am I my brother's keeper?"). The Lord stated that Abel's blood testified from the ground against Cain's murder (4:10).

8. Read Genesis 4:10. What did God communicate to Cain by saying Abel's blood cried out to Him?

9. Why is murder such a heinous sin?

Punishment

The Lord cursed Cain directly so that the ground would no longer yield anything for him (Gen. 3:17). The punishment was appropriate, since Cain had been a farmer (4:2, 12). Cain was forced to wander the earth, scrounging for food. He became a wanderer in the land of wandering. Cain complained (4:13), but he never repented. As a result, his face was hidden from the Lord (4:14), meaning that he never enjoyed fellowship with the Lord.

The Lord appointed a sign for Cain so that no one would slay him in vengeance for his murder of Abel. People were warned that should they kill Cain, they would experience a sevenfold vengeance from the Lord (4:15). The Lord's evenhandedness contrasted sharply with Cain's murder.

10. God showed Cain, an unbeliever, mercy by protecting him from a vengeful death. In what ways do unbelievers experience God's mercy today?

Adam and Eve had another son named Seth. "Seth" means "appointed one." Seth was appointed in the place of his dead brother, Abel (Gen. 4:25).

Noah's Piety

11. Do you agree that sin has never been more prevalent than now? Why?

Genesis 6:5–7, 11, and 12 provide a sobering assessment of the sinfulness of humanity. These verses clearly teach the total depravity of the human race. What a contrast with the "very good" of Genesis 1:31! After sin entered the world, people died. Sin exacted its heavy price.

Human sin also brought the animal kingdom under God's judgment (Gen. 6:7). Because the animals were under man's sinful dominion (compare that with God's original intention in 1:28), they were also under God's divine judgment. Our sin affected the animals. All creation groans, awaiting the final redemption (Rom. 8:20–22). In just a few short chapters, the story of the Old Testament makes it clear that humanity desperately needs God's mercy and grace.

One of the most important words for all of human history is the word "but" that begins Genesis 6:8. In the preceding verse, God was prepared to blot out all of humanity. *But* "Noah found grace in the eyes of the LORD." Noah pleased God, and he, like Enoch his ancestor, "walked with God" (6:9). Genesis 6:8 and 9 provide welcome relief from the monotonous genealogies. We learn that Noah pleased God ("found grace"), that he was righteous in the sight of God ("a just man"), that he maintained a blameless reputation among his contemporaries ("perfect in his generations"), and that he enjoyed fellowship with God ("walked with God"). The example of Noah teaches believers of every age that it is possible to please God even when they are encircled by sin.

The Flood

God explained to Noah that He was about to send a worldwide flood to destroy the earth. God instructed Noah to build an ark, to make it watertight, and to fill it with pairs of animals (6:13–22). Noah was also to bring on board extra animals that were clean for food and sacrifice (7:2; 8:20).

12. In what sense was the building of the ark over 120 years (6:3) a demonstration of God's patience and mercy?

The account of the Flood emphasizes Noah's obedience (6:22; 7:5). That Noah, his family, and the animals stayed in the ark for seven days after God closed the door but before He sent the Flood is most indicative of Noah's obedience (7:1, 4, 10). We can imagine all the people outside the ark laughing at crazy old Noah, rejecting the truth that God was mercifully granting them another week of life. For his part, Noah followed the plan of God, and he and those with him were saved (2 Pet. 2:5). Jesus taught that the people did not understand until the Flood came and washed them all away to their death (Matt. 24:37–39).

13. What are examples from your life of choosing obedience despite not experiencing immediate fulfillment of God's promises?

Noah clearly contrasted with the wicked people of his day. He obeyed God by faith, for in the pre-Flood world there was no rain (Gen. 2:5, 6). By taking God at His word, Noah believed in that which he had never seen, prepared the ark, condemned the world, and became an "heir of the righteousness" that comes by faith (Heb. 11:7).

We also see God revealing Himself in the Flood. We see His awesome power in submerging the earth. The floodwaters arose for forty days and nights (Gen. 7:4, 12, 17). The firmament water canopy collapsed, and the subterranean waters erupted (7:11). The mountains were covered, and all earth-dwelling creatures perished (7:20–23). The floodwaters reached their highest point after 150 days (7:24). Seventy-four days after the climax, the ark rested on the mountains of Ararat (8:4).

After having spent more than a year in the ark, Noah and his family and the animals left the ark (8:14–19). We see God's power in the destructive force of the Flood, and we see His power in the way He protected Noah and those who were with him.

We also see the patience and mercy of God. He did not send the Flood right away, but He allowed the earth 120 years to repent (6:3). Every day that Noah was required to build the massive ark was another opportunity for someone to repent. We also see God's mercy and grace in the way He delivered Noah and his family and the animals in the ark.

God's Covenant with Noah

God also showed His mercy in the promise represented by the rainbow (8:21, 22; 9:13) and in the covenant He made with Noah (6:18; 9:8–17). Although humanity is totally depraved, God promised that He would never again completely cover the dry land with water. The rainbow is the sign of the covenant that God made with Noah, with all his descendants, and with every living thing upon the earth. Therefore, we, as Noah's descendants, are beneficiaries of the Noahic Covenant.

14. How many of the generations from Noah have witnessed a rainbow?

15. How does this fact about rainbows help you understand the Noahic Covenant?

When God sends a storm cloud, He sees the rainbow. It stands as a sign of His promise that never again will He use water to destroy all flesh. The covenant is unconditional, meaning that God has bound Himself alone to ensure that the covenant is kept. It is a unilateral agreement. One day in the future, God will destroy this present earth in judgment. Since He has promised that He will not use water to destroy it, He will use fire instead (2 Pet. 3:4–7).

The People Build a Tower

As Noah's descendants journeyed eastward, they came to the plain of Shinar, the flat area between the Tigris and Euphrates Rivers. Shinar is the ancient name for Babylonia. The people settled there and determined to build a city and a tower. They did so with oven-baked clay bricks and tar mortar (Gen. 11:3). The fact that everyone spoke the same language and had the same culture made the building process possible (11:1).

Mankind's dialogue was similar to God's. They both said "let us" (11:4, 7). Genesis 11:5, right at the center of the story, serves as the transition by showing God coming down to the humans who were trying to build up to Him. In this way, the story uses subtle humor to draw a distinction between mankind's futile projects and plans and God's certain work.

The tower served three purposes (11:4). First, the people wanted its top to reach "heaven." Years later, the ziggurats of Babylon and Assyria were built for a similar purpose. These stepped pyramids hosted shrines to the gods of the heavens at their tops. The top of the tower of Babel would have had a room for their "god" with the planets, the sun, and the moon as prominent features in the design. We may assume, therefore, that the first purpose of the tower was to perpetuate a false religion based on worship involving the heavenly bodies. The builders of the tower of Babel, in essence, replaced God with a god they could personally define and manipulate.

16. What personal desires lay at the heart of worshiping a god that can be personally defined and manipulated?

Second, the people at Babel wanted to make a name for themselves. This means that they wanted to establish their fame, their reputation, by completing that massive building project. They intended to make a shrine not only to the heavens, but also to human strength and ingenuity.

17. Read Psalm 19:1–4. God made the heavens as a testimony to *His* strength and ingenuity. How do they compare to the tower of Babel, a testimony to humanity's strength and ingenuity?

Third, the tower builders wanted to halt the spread of humanity throughout the earth. This effort was a violation of God's directive (Gen. 9:1). Apparently humanity believed God was irrelevant and powerless.

God knew that a human race united in language and purpose would commit unbridled evil (11:6). Therefore, the Lord came down and confused the people's language. Thus, the people could no longer understand one another. In a play on words, the name "Babel" is similar to the Hebrew word for "confuse." The confused people stopped building the city and tower and scattered themselves by language groups throughout the earth.

We see God's judgment in that He confused the people's language. But that act was also merciful. Imagine the debauchery and rebellion that would have developed had the people of Babel continued to live as one people.

Making It Personal

18. What do you believe about God's judgment of sin?

19. Does your life match what you say you believe? Do you take sin seriously? Do you expect God to lovingly discipline you if you persist in sin? Explain.

20. What changes might you need to make in light of God's judgment of sin?

21. Name someone who needs to hear about God's merciful offer of salvation.

22. How could you use the accounts covered in this lesson as a witnessing tool?

23. Memorize Genesis 6:5 and 8.

Revelation and Redemption in the Days of the Patriarchs

God is always faithful despite our circumstances.

Genesis 12; 15–18

"And he believed in the LORD; and he counted it to him for righteousness" (Genesis 15:6).

Cell-phone service, United States Postal Service, your coffee maker, your car, dog, cat, other drivers. We all label such things and people as either faithful or unfaithful. No one likes when something or someone proves unfaithful.

Unfaithful is a label some people put on God. But a careful study of His Word proves otherwise.

Getting Started

1. What must be true of someone or something in order for you to consider them faithful?

2. What evidences of God's faithfulness are meaningful to you?

This lesson highlights God's faithfulness with the patriarchs. We serve the same faithful God today.

Searching the Scriptures

This lesson considers the covenant that God made with Abraham—an example of a royal grant covenant. In the Abrahamic Covenant, God made irrevocable promises to Abraham and to Abraham's descendants. The Abrahamic Covenant is unconditional, irrevocable, and permanent, but its blessings are conditional in that Abraham's descendants through Isaac were to practice circumcision; otherwise, they would be cut off from the nation and cut off from God's blessings.

3. What are some examples of irrevocable agreements in our culture?

4. Why do you think irrevocable agreements are rare?

5. What does this type of covenant reveal about God?

God's Call of Abraham

Before Abraham (or Abram as he was called at the time) lived in Haran, while he was still in Ur of Mesopotamia (Gen. 11:31; Acts 7:2), God commanded him to leave his relatives and home (Gen. 12:1).

God promised Abraham that (1) He would make him into a great nation, (2) He would bless him, (3) He would make his name great, (4) He would bless those who blessed him, (5) He would curse those that cursed him, and (6) all families of the earth would be blessed in him (12:2, 3). Abraham took God at His word and journeyed to Canaan. When Abraham passed through the land, the Lord promised to give it to him (12:7; 13:14–17; 15:6, 16, 17).

Soon Abraham began experiencing some of the covenant promises. For example, the Lord struck Pharaoh and his household with a plague because Pharaoh had unwittingly taken Sarah, Abraham's wife, into his harem (12:17). Also, God blessed Abraham and his allies when they defeated Chedorlaomer and rescued Abraham's nephew Lot (14:13–16, 24).

Genesis 15 records an impressive covenant renewal ceremony. Abraham was still childless. He suggested that God approve the adoption of Eliezer as Abraham's heir (15:2–4). God promised Abraham that he would have a son (15:4) and that he would have descendants beyond numbering, like the stars of the night sky (15:5).

6. Read Genesis 15:1–6. What did God count as righteousness in Abraham's life?

7. What did the aging, childless Abraham learn about what pragmatics have to do with trusting God will be faithful to His word?

God's Unconditional Covenant with Abraham

Abraham asked God for some confirmation of the promise. So God instructed Abraham to gather some animals and to divide their carcasses, except for the birds, into two halves. Abraham then took the divided animal carcasses and laid each half opposite the other (15:8–10). Carrion came to eat the carcasses; Abraham drove the birds away (15:11). As the sun descended, Abraham fell into a deep sleep. God spoke to

Abraham and told him that his descendants would be enslaved for four hundred years, that God would bring them out with many possessions, that Abraham would die in peace, and that his descendants would eventually settle in the Promised Land (15:13–16).

When it was very dark, God appeared in the form of a smoking oven and flaming torch (15:17). The Lord passed through the divided animal carcasses in a covenant renewal ceremony (15:17). Normally, when people made covenants like this, they would pass between the divided carcasses together. As they walked, they would swear oaths to each other to the effect that if they broke the covenant, they would become like the divided carcasses (Jer. 34:18–20). In fact to "make" a covenant in Hebrew is literally to "cut" a covenant.

In Genesis 15, the Lord cut the covenant differently. He alone passed between the carcass parts. His unaccompanied movement emphasized the unconditional nature of the Abrahamic Covenant. The Lord obliged only Himself; Abraham was not required to swear anything for the covenant to become operational. God promised to give the land to Abraham's descendants (Gen. 15:18). No stipulations were included; no conditions were required.

8. Why would God make His covenant with Abraham unconditional?

Similar unconditional language appears in Genesis 17:4–8. However, in verse 9, God stated, "Thou shalt keep my covenant therefore, thou, and thy seed after thee in their generations." Circumcision was the "token of the covenant" (15:11). This token makes the Abrahamic Covenant appear, at first glance, to carry a condition—the condition of circumcision. Actually, the Abrahamic Covenant is unconditional in its operation; but, for a person to enter into its blessings, circumcision was required.

This may seem confusing, but salvation is similar. Christ died and rose again to provide salvation for all. The offer of salvation is fully operational. Nevertheless, to enter into the blessings of salvation, an individual person must believe that Christ died for him or her. Therefore, the gift of salvation is unconditionally offered, but it is conditionally received by faith.

9. Read Genesis 18:16—19:29. How does this passage develop the theme of God's faithfulness to His promises to Abraham, particularly to be a blessing to all people?

10. Read Genesis 22:1–19. How does this passage develop the theme of God's faithfulness to His promises to Abraham?

Another apparent condition to the Abrahamic Covenant appears in Genesis 18:19. This verse acknowledges that Abraham would command his children and household to keep the way of the Lord—"that the LORD may bring upon Abraham that which he hath spoken of him." God's promises of the land, descendants, and blessings are unconditional, but to enjoy them, a descendant of Abraham must follow the Lord as Abraham did.

A third apparent condition to the Abrahamic Covenant appears in Genesis 22:16–18. These verses record the message from the angel of the Lord who called unto Abraham from Heaven (22:15). Since Abraham did not withhold his son Isaac, but was willing to believe God and obey Him, God would bless Abraham. Furthermore, in Abraham's seed, "all the nations of the earth" will be blessed because Abraham "obeyed [God's] voice" (22:18).

Actually, these verses record a simple reaffirmation of the covenant plus the promise that Abraham's "seed shall possess the gate of his enemies" (22:17; also see 24:60). Following Abraham's extraordinary demonstration of faith and obedience, God steadied the old man's nerves by reassuring Abraham of His original intentions and by providing some minor expansion on earlier themes. That the covenant is unconditional appears in this passage, for the angel of the Lord declares, "By myself have I sworn" (22:16).

God Deals with Abraham's Descendants

One helpful way to study the remainder of the book of Genesis is to study it within the context of the Abrahamic Covenant. The Old Testament explains (1) how God made Abraham's descendants into a great nation, (2) how He blessed Abraham's descendants, and (3) how He blessed those who blessed Israel and cursed those who cursed Israel. The New Testament explains how God blessed all the families of the earth through the one special descendent of Abraham, the Lord Jesus Christ.

11. What Old Testament accounts evidence Abraham's descendants became a great nation?

12. What Old Testament accounts show God blessing and cursing those who did the same to Israel?

13. How does the New Testament present Jesus as the descendant of Abraham Who blesses all people?

Isaac

14. Read Genesis 26:2–4. What promises does God reaffirm with Isaac?

Genesis includes an extensive chapter on the marriage of Isaac (chap. 24) because the Abrahamic Covenant promises blessings to and through the descendants of Abraham. Abraham's son, Isaac, therefore needed the right wife (24:3, 4). Isaac's marriage to Rebekah proved important for the perpetuation of the family tree. The Lord then reaffirmed the covenant with Isaac (26:2–4).

The Lord blessed the marriage of Isaac and Rebekah with twins, and a dilemma presented itself. Through which twin would God's blessings be perpetuated? Rebekah inquired of the Lord for an answer (25:22, 23). The Lord told her that the older, Esau, would serve the younger, Jacob. Rebekah and Jacob settled for intrigue to swindle the blessing (chap. 27), even though the Lord had already promised it to Jacob. The birthright (25:31) and blessing (27:4) meant so much to Jacob because he believed in the Abrahamic Covenant.

15. What did Jacob reveal about his belief in God's faithfulness by swindling the birthright and blessing from his brother?

Esau despised his birthright (25:34) and married pagan Canaanite women (26:34, 35; 27:46). After the deception, Isaac confirmed the blessing of Abraham upon Jacob (Gen. 28:1–4).

Jacob

16. Read Genesis 28:10–15. What promises does God reaffirm with Jacob?

After receiving the blessing by deception, Jacob journeyed to his mother's homeland—running from Esau and looking for a wife. On the way, the Lord appeared to Jacob in a dream at Bethel (28:10–15). In this dream, the Lord reconfirmed the Abrahamic Covenant with Jacob. The Lord revealed Himself to Jacob as the God of his father and grandfather. He promised the land to Jacob and to his descendants (28:13). God also promised a multitude of descendants for Jacob. He added, "In thy seed shall all the families of the earth be blessed" (28:14). The Lord utilized language reminiscent of Genesis 12:2 and 3.

Jacob returned to the Promised Land with a large family. On the way, he received word that his brother, Esau, was coming to meet him with four hundred men. Jacob was afraid, so he prayed to God for deliverance from his brother (32:6, 7).

17. Read Genesis 32:9–12. Why would Jacob be afraid when he already had God's promise to make of his descendants a great nation?

Jacob claimed the promises of the Abrahamic Covenant (32:9–12). Essentially, Jacob prayed, "Lord, You promised that my descendants would be numberless, please protect my family in accordance with Your promise."

When Jacob returned to Bethel, the Lord appeared to him again and reassured him with the promises of the Abrahamic Covenant (35:11–13). This time, though, the Lord mentioned that "kings shall come out of thy loins" (35:11). This additional promise foreshadowed that the nation Israel would eventually become a kingdom.

Toward the end of his life, as Jacob journeyed to Egypt to meet his long-lost son Joseph, the Lord appeared to Jacob and reconfirmed the Abrahamic Covenant one more time (46:3). Traveling to Egypt and away from the Promised Land was another reason for Jacob to fear that God's promises would not come to pass. God's personal words to Jacob had to be reassuring to him.

Clearly, the covenant plays a major role in God's self-revelation and work of redemption. God revealed Himself as a God Who makes promises and Who keeps promises. God is faithful.

God also revealed that He will bless all the families of the earth through the one family of Abraham. God is a redeemer, and the Redeemer would come through the line of Abraham. Genesis 3:15 reveals that the Promised One would come from the woman. After Genesis 12, it becomes clearer that the Promised One would come through the line of Abraham.

Joseph

Following the theme of the Abrahamic Covenant, the story of Joseph is also a story about how God keeps His promises. God promised Abraham that He would make his descendants into a great nation. However, the famine in Canaan would have brought an end to Jacob's family were it not for Joseph's provisions. Although Israel's sons sold their brother Joseph into slavery in Egypt, God was the One Who actually sent Joseph ahead of his brothers "to preserve life" (45:5).

Psalm 105:16–24 unmistakably describe God's plan and sovereignty. God "called for a famine," so He "sent a man," Joseph, "before them" into Egypt (105:16, 17). God's words, that is, His command, tried Joseph (105:19). The rejection by his brothers and the false accusation by Potiphar's wife tried Joseph and prepared him to be ruler in Egypt. When the time was just right, Pharaoh promoted Joseph. Joseph worked to store the grain for the seven lean years. Joseph's administration permitted his family to go to Egypt and to sojourn there close to Joseph and close to the stored grain. God "increased his people greatly" so that they became a mighty nation (105:24). God showed Himself faithful to Abraham and faithful to his family and descendants.

Making It Personal

God is always faithful to His promises and to His attributes. There is never a time when God stops being loving, just, omnipresent, or any of His other attributes. We can count on Him to be the same even when our circumstances seem to indicate that He has stopped caring for us or that He has lost control of our circumstances.

18. What circumstances seemed to indicate that God was being unfaithful to the patriarchs?

19. Why can't we look at our circumstances as a test of God's faithfulness?

20. What circumstances in your life have tested your trust in God's faithfulness?

21. What has God done to assure you of His faithfulness?

22. What could you do to remember God's faithfulness this week?

23. Memorize Genesis 15:6.

Revelation and Redemption at the Exodus

God's revelation of Himself informs our response to Him.

Exodus 2; 3; 14; 15; 19; 20

**"And the LORD said, I have surely seen the afflic-
tion of my people which are in Egypt, and have
heard their cry by reason of their taskmasters;
for I know their sorrows; and I am come down to
deliver them out of the hand of the Egyptians,
and to bring them up out of the land unto a
good land and a large, unto a land flowing with
milk and honey" (Exodus 3:7, 8a).**

I n Chicago, Illinois, it is illegal to fish in your pajamas. In
Greene, New York, it is illegal to eat peanuts and walk back-
wards on a sidewalk during a concert. In Omaha, Nebraska, a child's
parents could be arrested if the child burps in church.

Getting Started

1. What other nonsensical municipal codes are you aware of?

2. When have you been frustrated with your city's laws?

One of the Bible's primary objectives is to teach us about God. Every part of the Bible, including the Law, communicates to us about God.

Searching the Scriptures

Developing the skill of learning about God by considering various Bible accounts and genres is an important skill for believers.

God had kept the first part of His promise to Abraham. Abraham's descendants were strangers in the land of Egypt. And the Israelites served the Egyptians, who neglected and afflicted them for four hundred years (Gen. 15:13).

As the book of Exodus opens, we read that God would also keep the second part of His promise to Abraham. God would judge Egypt and bring His people Israel out of Egypt with "great substance" (15:14).

Birth of Moses

3. If you didn't know how Exodus began would you anticipate finding God's people enslaved in Egypt? Why?

4. What does God's use of "bad" circumstances to accomplish His purposes teach us about Him?

Moses was born in exciting days in that God's promises were about to be fulfilled. Moses was also born in dangerous days for Pharaoh had commanded that every Israelite baby boy was to be abandoned to the Nile River (Exod. 1:22; Acts 7:19).

Moses' mother hid him for three months then waterproofed his little reed basket and put him in the Nile (Exod. 2:2, 3). She had Moses' sister watch the basket from a distance.

Pharaoh's daughter, perhaps Princess Hatshepsut, saw Moses' reed basket (Exod. 2:5). Moses' weeping moved Pharaoh's daughter to compassion. She adopted Moses as her own son (2:6–10; Acts 7:21).

Moses' rescue from the water of the Nile foreshadowed God's deliverance of Israel through the water of the Red Sea. Moses' mother's nurturing, while paid by Pharaoh's daughter, foreshadowed God's provisions for Israel at the expense of Egypt.

At the age of forty, Moses went out and saw the afflictions of his people. By faith, he identified himself with Israel, a slave nation, instead of with the Egyptians (Heb. 11:24, 25).

Moses saw an Egyptian master beating an Israelite slave, so Moses killed the Egyptian. He hid the body in the sand, but the incident came to Pharaoh's attention. Moses fled to Midian (Exod. 2:11–15). God had not yet prepared Moses to be the ruler of His people. And his fellow Israelites questioned his authority (compare Exod. 2:14 with Acts 7:27). Moses feared that he had messed up God's plan with his impatience. Therefore, he fled from the king until such time as God would use him to redeem His people from slavery.

After forty years, Moses was no longer so eager to lead the people. Self-doubt had replaced his self-confidence. Nevertheless, his faith in the invisible God sustained him through the years (Heb. 11:27).

In Midian, the Lord prepared Moses for the years that he would spend leading Israel in the wilderness wanderings. Moses eventually married and had children (Exod. 2:21, 22; 18:3, 4).

5. Why does God sometimes use the passage of time to prepare leaders?

Call of Moses

In Exodus 3 God called Moses from a burning bush that was not consumed by the fire. Moses answered, "Here am I" (3:4). God then revealed Himself to Moses as the holy One, the God of the Patriarchs, as the concerned and compassionate One, and as the faithful Lord Who keeps His promises (3:5–8).

6. Read Exodus 3:1–10. How would you expect Moses to respond to God's call in light of God's revelation of Himself to Moses?

7. Read Exodus 3:11. What was wrong with Moses' focus?

Moses considered God's self-revelation to be insufficient for Israel (3:11, 13). God promised Moses that He would be with him (3:12). God then revealed Himself to Moses as the great I AM. God is the "I AM THAT I AM"; He is the One Who owes His existence to no other (3:14). God also reiterated the promises of old (compare Exod. 3:19–22 with Gen. 15:14). After some more objections (Exod. 4), the eighty-year-old Moses acquiesced.

8. Read Exodus 4:1–17. How much did Moses' perception of himself and his assessment of his abilities matter to God? Why was that?

Plagues

Moses met Pharaoh and said, "Let my people go" (Exod. 5:1). Pharaoh increased his expectations for the Israelite slaves. As a result, the Israelites were in anguish for their cruel bondage (5:6–9, 19–21; 6:9). Moses should not have been surprised. God had promised that only with great judgments would He bring Israel out of slavery (7:1–5). This, then, is the background for the ten plagues (7:14—12:33).

The ten plagues revealed God both to Israel and to Egypt. God showed Himself as Almighty and the gods of Egypt as powerless.

The Lord provided a foreshadowing of what was to come. He called Israel His "firstborn" son (4:22, 23). The plagues culminated with the death of each firstborn. The firstborn of Israel were protected from the death angel in every home where, by faith, the family put the blood on the doorframe (12:7).

The Passover celebration is a beautiful picture of the sacrifice of Jesus Christ on the cross. As the perfect Lamb of God, Jesus shed His blood to satisfy God's righteous demands concerning our sin. By His blood we receive forgiveness; God's wrath is not poured out on us.

9. What can we learn about God by considering the ten plagues?

Israel obeyed God, and He smote the firstborn of Egypt (12:28, 29). Pharaoh called for Moses and Aaron that very night. He told the Israelites to go and worship God.

All the Egyptians urged the Israelites to go with haste. They gave the Israelites gold, silver, jewels, and fancy clothing (12:31–36). Later the Israelites were able to use the treasures of Egypt to build the tabernacle in the wilderness.

Red Sea Crossing

As the children of Israel left Egypt, the Lord led them to double back (14:2). Pharaoh concluded that the Israelites were "entangled" in the wilderness (14:3). God hardened Pharaoh's heart and Pharaoh pursued Israel. This allowed God to deliver Israel and show Egypt one more time that He is God (14:4, 8, 17, 18). When the Israelites saw Pharaoh's pursuing chariots, they were "sore afraid" (14:10). The Israelites bemoaned that Moses had ever rescued them from slavery (14:12).

10. Read Exodus 14:10–12. At whom did the people of Israel point their blaming fingers?

11. Read Exodus 14:13, 14. What was Moses' answer to their finger pointing and fear?

12. Why does adversity often cause people to doubt God's plans?

The Exodus, culminating with the crossing of the Red Sea, proclaimed God's redemptive concern so vividly that its power and clarity is surpassed only in the redemption provided by Christ's death at Calvary. The Old Testament story of redemption shines clearest here.

God redeemed Israel from slavery with finality (14:13b). First, He moved the pillar of cloud from before the Israelites to their rear guard to block the approach of the Egyptians and to provide light for Israel for the crossing but darkness for the Egyptians (14:19, 20). The pillars of cloud and fire were constant signs of God's presence.

Second, the Lord caused "a strong east wind" to blow all night so that the waters of the Red Sea were divided (14:21). Third, the Israelites crossed through the Red Sea on dry ground (14:22). Fourth, the Egyptians pursued the Israelites into the sea (14:23). Fifth, before dawn, in the darkest hours of the night, the Lord began to judge Egypt. He took off their chariot wheels and sent the heaped waters crashing back (14:24–28).

The Egyptians were afraid, but it was too late. By the morning light, the Israelites saw the "Egyptians dead upon the sea shore" (14:30). Israel also "saw that great work which the LORD did upon the Egyptians: and the people feared the LORD, and believed the LORD, and his servant Moses" (14:31).

God showed Himself so great and awesome that Moses and Miriam and all of Israel sang a great hymn of deliverance (15:1–21). The heart of the hymn appears in verse 11. This central verse teaches that God is unique, glorious in His holiness, awe-inspiring in His praises, and that

He accomplishes wonderful things.

From the Red Sea, the Israelites journeyed south and east to the southernmost region of the Sinai desert. The Lord led Moses and the people to Mount Sinai (also known as Mount Horeb; Deut. 5:2)—the same place where God had earlier revealed Himself to Moses (Exod. 3:12).

Sinaitic Covenant

At Mount Sinai, the Lord made another covenant with Israel. It is called either the Sinaitic or the Mosaic Covenant.

Unlike the Noahic and Abrahamic Covenants, which were unconditional and permanent, the Sinaitic Covenant was conditional and temporal.

13. What could we learn about God by considering the fact that He made a conditional, temporal covenant with Israel?

The Sinaitic Covenant began with a history of God's benevolence (19:4) and continued with the stipulations. The stipulations were to "obey" God and to "keep" the covenantal requirements. The Sinaitic Covenant concluded with promises based on obedience to the covenant (19:5, 6). The people then ratified the Sinaitic Covenant. All of Israel answered in unison, "All that the LORD hath spoken we will do" (19:8; 24:3, 7).

Clearly, the Sinaitic Covenant differed from the Noahic and Abrahamic Covenants. The Noahic Covenant was established "for perpetual generations" (Gen. 9:12), and the Abrahamic "for ever" (13:15). These were permanent covenants. The Sinaitic Covenant was temporary. Its legal requirements were also temporary.

The New Testament teaches this temporal nature of the Sinaitic Covenant (Heb. 8:6—10:8). The fact that God promised a New Covenant proves that He intended the old Sinaitic Covenant to be temporal (Jer. 31:31–34; Heb. 8:7, 8). The New Covenant is better because it is based on the blood and priesthood of Christ, not on the blood of animals or on the Aaronic priesthood (Heb. 9:11–14; 10:1, 2, 10–12).

14. Read Hebrews 10:1. Put into your own words the fact that the Law (Sinaitic Covenant) is a shadow of the blessings found in Jesus Christ.

The Sabbath became the sign of the covenant between God and Israel at Sinai (Exod. 31:12–17). The rainbow in the storm cloud was the sign of the Noahic Covenant. The rite of circumcision was the sign of the Abrahamic Covenant.

Law

The Sinaitic Covenant provided the context for understanding the laws of Moses. The laws are the stipulations, or the obligations, of the Sinaitic Covenant. If Israel wanted God's blessings, then Israel was required to keep the laws. The Ten Commandments (Exod. 20:3–17), written on the two tables of stone by God Himself, provided the heart of these covenantal requirements. The rest of the law (Exod. 19—40; Lev. 1—27; Num. 1:1—10:10) provided additional requirements, all springing from the core Ten Commandments. The laws, then, are not requirements for us New Testament believers because we are not partners in the Sinaitic Covenant. Besides, the old Sinaitic Covenant is no longer operative; it has vanished away (Heb. 8:6–13).

While most of the commands in the Ten Commandments are repeated in some form in the New Testament, the conditional Sinaitic covenant is not tied to those New Testament commands. In this current dispensation of grace, we obey God out of love and appreciation for Him. We cannot claim the promises of blessings attached to the Law of Moses as our own.

The Law of Moses does have value for us in that God reveals Himself throughout the law.

15. What truths does God reveal about Himself through the Ten Commandments?

Although the law was inadequate and temporal (Rom. 6:14; 8:2; Gal. 5:18), "the law is holy, and the commandment holy, and just, and good" (Rom. 7:12) because it revealed God and His expectations for Israel.

16. How might thinking of the law as a self-revelation of God change your way of studying it?

Soon after Israel ratified the covenant at Sinai (Exod. 19:8; 24:3, 7), the nation broke the covenant. While Moses was on the summit (24:12–18), the nation began worshiping another god and committing adultery (32:6).

No wonder the Lord lamented that Israel had "turned aside quickly out of the way" (32:8). When Moses neared the camp, he broke the two tablets of stone and thereby symbolized the way that Israel had broken the covenant stipulations (32:19).

The Lord, however, is merciful, gracious, patient, good, and true (34:5–7). Moses made two new stone tablets as God instructed. God again called the people to obedience (34:10, 11). This renewed call served as a covenant renewal ceremony.

This pattern of commitment to obedience, disobedience, God's punishment, Israel's repentance, and renewal of commitment repeated itself over and over again throughout the Old Testament. The cycle reveals the holiness, justice, mercy, patience, and faithfulness of God.

Making It Personal

17. How has today's lesson increased your ability to learn about God by considering narratives and Old Testament law?

18. How does the opportunity to connect circumstances from your life to these truths increase your appreciation for Old Testament study?

19. What was a surprising insight or helpful reminder about God from today's lesson?

20. How should these lessons impact your life of faith? What is one specific thing you can do this week to respond to God's self-revelation studied today?

21. Memorize Exodus 3:7 and 8a.

Revelation and Redemption in the Pre-Kingdom Days

*God is faithful both to bless
and discipline believers.*

Deut. 29; Josh. 6—8; 14; Judg. 2

"Keep therefore the words of this covenant, and do them, that ye may prosper in all that ye do" (Deuteronomy 29:9).

Given a choice, most young kids would select lenient parents who rarely or never disciplined them. But their choice would end up hurting them more than any discipline ever would.

No one likes discipline, but everyone needs it. For us as believers, discipline is essential and valuable. God is faithful. So we can count on Him to lovingly discipline us.

Getting Started

1. Do you think demonstrations of faithfulness are usually positive or negative actions?

2. How can a negative or disciplinary action be an example of faithfulness?

This lesson is focused on God's faithfulness demonstrated in both His blessing and cursing of Israel.

Searching the Scriptures

Wilderness Wanderings

Israel spent eleven months at Mount Sinai. Then the Lord led Israel to the borders of the Promised Land. The journey, though short, was filled with unbelief and bitter complaining (Num. 11—14). As a result of the complaining at Kadesh-Barnea, God condemned the people to forty years of wandering in the wilderness (14:33, 34). Their unbelief and rebellion transformed an eleven-day journey into one that lasted forty years. The years were filled with more rebellion and complaining. Even Moses lost his temper (20:10–12).

During the wanderings, the Lord revealed more of His laws and expectations to His people (Num. 18; 19; 27—30). Finally, the younger generation arrived again at the borders of the Promised Land and even conquered the lands on the east side of the Jordan. The people pitched their tents by the Jordan River in the plains of Moab.

The final chapters of Numbers provide the legislation regarding the tribal and inheritance allotments of the Promised Land (33:50—36:13).

3. Does God's judgment and discipline reflect poorly on God's faithfulness? Why?

4. Read Hebrews 12:3–11. How do these verses communicate that God's judgment and discipline are evidences of His faithfulness?

The entire book of Deuteronomy, which records the sermons that Moses preached to the people during the last months of his life, provides legislation that prepared Israel for a settled life in the Promised Land.

The structure of much of the book of Deuteronomy resembles the structure of a suzerainty treaty. Early on, Moses recorded a history of God's past protection and provision (Deut. 1:6—4:43). Then Moses wrote God's stipulations and expectations (4:44—26:19). These are followed by the directions for a covenant ratification ceremony to take place in the Promised Land, complete with a recitation of blessings and curses for obedience and disobedience (27:1—30:20).

Israel was required to make the sign for this covenant by building an altar of uncut stones, covering the stones with white plaster, offering a burnt offering on them, and writing the law stipulations "very plainly" on the stones (27:4–8). This covenant is sometimes called the Palestinian Covenant, the Covenant of the Plains of Moab, or the Deuteronomic Covenant.

The book of Deuteronomy closes with the final words and death of Moses (Deut. 31—34).

Deuteronomic (Palestinian) Covenant

The Deuteronomic Covenant made on the plains of Moab, near the border of the Promised Land, differed from the one made at Mount Sinai, or Horeb (29:1).

Deuteronomy 29 presents this covenant in summary form. It began with a history of God's past protection and provision (29:2–8). It included the stipulation of obedience (29:9). It encompassed all the covenant participants: those standing there that day (29:14) and those who should come in subsequent generations (29:22). And it ended with threats of curses for disobedience (29:23–28).

Both the Sinaitic and Deuteronomic Covenants were conditional. That is, both carried the stipulation of obedience. Although there is much overlap, the two differed in their emphases. The Sinaitic Covenant expected obedience to a law that sprang from the Ten Commandments. The law governed a person's time, possessions, relationships—the person's very life.

The Deuteronomic Covenant governed life on the land. The covenant at Sinai taught Israel how to live. The covenant in Deuteronomy taught Israel how to dwell. If Israel kept the Deuteronomic Covenant, then God would bless her life on the land. If Israel disobeyed, then God would curse her life on the land; and if she persisted in disobedience, God would remove her from the land.

It is true that the land belongs to Israel forever, unconditionally, by virtue of the Abrahamic Covenant (Gen. 13:15). However, for any one generation of Israel to enjoy the unconditional promise of the Abrahamic Covenant, it had to obey the Deuteronomic Covenant.

5. What word would you use to describe how Israel should have responded to God's faithfulness revealed in both the Sinaitic and Deuteronomic Covenants?

After Moses died Joshua became the leader of Israel (Deut. 34:7–9; Josh. 1:1, 2). Joshua sent two spies secretly to Jericho, having learned from the negative experience at Kadesh Barnea forty years earlier (2:1).

Joshua led the people to cross the Jordan in a manner reminiscent of the Red Sea crossing (Josh. 3:13, 16; 4:18). The Lord used the Jordan crossing to increase Joshua's prestige as a leader (4:14).

Joshua, like Moses, had his own contact with the Lord (5:13–15).

Israel Conquers Canaan

Essentially, Joshua led the people of Israel to conquer the land in three major campaigns. First, Israel conquered central Canaan (Josh. 6—8). Next, Israel conquered southern Canaan (Josh. 9; 10). Finally, Israel conquered northern Canaan (Josh. 11). After the major Canaanite strongholds fell to Joshua, it was up to each tribe to further secure its individual allotment.

6. How did God demonstrate His faithfulness through Israel's victory over Jericho (Josh. 6)?

7. How did God demonstrate His faithfulness through Israel's defeat at Ai (Josh. 7)?

8. How might God show His faithfulness through the defeats in our lives?

The Lord enabled Israel to conquer the land. When Israel obeyed, the Lord granted the victory. When Israel disobeyed, the Lord withheld His aid, and Israel suffered defeat. The contrast vividly appears in the different military outcomes at Jericho and Ai (Josh. 6; 7). God revealed His holiness and faithfulness in the two incidents. God keeps His promises and punishes sin.

At Jericho, God tested Israel's faith. He required Israel to march around the city once a day for six days with seven priests blowing on seven rams-horn trumpets (6:3, 4, 8, 9, 13, 14). The people, however, were to remain silent (6:10). On the seventh day, Israel was to march around the city seven times. At the end, the priests were to blow a long blast, and all the people were to shout (6:15, 16). Then, the walls were to "fall down flat" (6:5). Every soldier would go straight into the city.

God placed the city of Jericho under His ban. It was to be utterly destroyed. No one was allowed to keep any plunder for himself (6:17–19).

"So the people shouted" at the end of the long blast at the end of the seventh march at the end of the seventh day, and the walls fell flat just as the Lord had promised (6:20).

Joshua saved Rahab and her household because she had saved the spies (6:25). Joshua burned the city with fire and put all the valuable metals into the Lord's treasury (6:24). The battle at Jericho showed that God keeps His word and that He rewards those who, by faith, obey Him.

9. What are some evidences of our faith in God?

10. What are some evidences that we are not exhibiting faith in God?

At the first battle of Ai, Israel trusted in her own strength and was soundly defeated. Joshua's intelligence reconnaissance recommended a force of only two or three thousand men since the city was small. Joshua sent the men without first enquiring of the Lord. The men of Ai smote the Israelites and killed about thirty-six men. Joshua complained (7:3–7).

The Lord responded to Joshua, "Get thee up" because "Israel hath sinned" (7:10, 11). He commanded Joshua to sanctify Israel, to set her apart from the accursed thing. Someone had taken plunder from the city of Jericho, so Israel could not stand against her enemies (7:13).

The next day, Joshua gathered the leaders of Israel. The Lord delineated the culprit—Achan—by tribe, family, and household (7:16–18). Achan had stolen a Babylonian garment, five pounds of silver, and one-and-a-quarter pounds of gold. He had hidden the items beneath his tent, implicating his family in the concealment (7:21). Therefore, Israel stoned him, his family, and all his animals. They then burned him and all that he had, including the stolen plunder, and piled stones upon the ashes (7:25, 26).

The Lord told Joshua to take courage and to send all the fighting men of Israel after Ai; He promised plunder to Israel this time. Too bad Achan was not more patient; he could have received legal plunder at Ai (8:1, 2)!

Joshua set two ambushes (8:3, 4, 13). He feigned retreat with his main force and thereby drew the soldiers out from Ai and Bethel (8:15–17). The ambushers took the city and burned it while Joshua turned back on the enemy. The army of Ai found itself completely surrounded (8:21, 22). All the men of Ai died that day (8:25).

God gave a complete victory to His people when they obeyed Him and kept His covenant .

Division of and Dwelling in Canaan

Much of the book of Joshua deals with the division of the Promised Land among the twelve tribes (Joshua 13—21). This section may appear lackluster, but it is a record of God's faithfulness to Israel. He had promised the land to His people, and He made good on His promise. The book closes with some of Joshua's sermons of encouragement (chaps. 22—24).

The book of Joshua closes with another testimony to the faithfulness of God: Israel buried the bones of Joseph (24:32; also see Genesis

50:25 and Hebrews 11:22).

11. Who do you know who has demonstrated faith in God over many years? With what behaviors do they evidence their faith?

Joshua led Israel in a covenant renewal ceremony at Shechem before all the people returned to their inheritances (Josh. 24:22–28). As long as Joshua and his generation lived, the people served the Lord (24:31; Judg. 2:8–10). However, the tribes of Israel did not utterly drive out the Canaanites from their allotments (cf. Judg. 1:19, 21, 27, 29).

12. Read Deuteronomy 7:2; 12:3; and Judges 2:1, 2. In what terms did the Angel of the Lord lament Israel's failure?

After Joshua's generation died, Israel did evil before the Lord (Judg. 2:11). They turned their backs on the Patriarch's God, Who had redeemed them from slavery, and Who had brought them into the Promised Land. Because they had broken the covenant, God's hand would be against them for evil—just as He had sworn He would do in the Deuteronomic Covenant (2:15). Because Israel broke the Deuteronomic Covenant, God refused to drive the Canaanites completely out from the land (Judg. 2:20–23). This means that although Israel dwelt in the Promised Land, she did not dwell alone. She began intermarrying with the pagans around her (3:6).

13. Why might people fail to completely obey God?

Judges records the downward cycles that ensued. The cycles had six points: (1) Israel broke the covenant stipulations, (2) she was defeated and oppressed by her enemy, (3) she repented of her sin and called out to God, (4) God raised up a judge to deliver, (5) the judge delivered and led Israel, (6) she served the Lord, enjoyed rest, but eventually arrived back at point 1 following the death of the judge. The book of Ruth is a testimony that individual faithfulness is possible in the midst of a disobedient culture.

Making It Personal

Sometimes we think God exists to protect us from harm, make our lives easy, keep us happy, and fulfill all our dreams and wishes. When we experience difficulties we might conclude that God has failed. Instead we need to trust that He is always faithful.

We should consider that perhaps it us who has failed and that God is faithfully using circumstances to draw us back to Him.

14. Before studying this lesson, how often did you consider God's disciplining works as evidence of His faithfulness?

15. How has your perspective changed?

16. How should God's faithfulness to discipline you motivate your obedience to Him?

17. How can you encourage others to more consistently remember God's faithfulness?

18. Memorize Deuteronomy 29:9.

Lesson 7

Revelation and Redemption in the United Kingdom

God is the Great King to Whom our submission and reverence is due.

1 Samuel 7—9; 15; 16; 2 Samuel 7; 1 Kings 11

"My covenant will I not break, nor alter the thing that is gone out of my lips. Once have I sworn by my holiness that I will not lie unto David. His seed shall endure for ever, and his throne as the sun before me" (Psalm 89:34–36).

King Henry VIII is perhaps one of the most well-known kings, though generally not for good reasons. He married six times, beheaded two of his wives, and was the primary instigator of the English Reformation, turning England into a Protestant country. Lustful, egotistical, harsh, and insecure were common descriptions of the king, particularly as he neared the end of his reign.

Getting Started

1. Name some famous kings from history. Why do they stand out in your memory?

2. What makes a king either good or bad?

This lesson focuses both on God as Israel's king and on the human kings who were to administer God's theocratic rule of Israel.

Searching the Scriptures

Israel Requests a King

The first seven chapters of 1 Samuel would form a fitting appendix to the book of Judges. The chapters record the misfortunes that ensued when Israel forsook the covenant: the Philistines captured of the ark of the covenant (4:10, 11), Eli the high priest died (4:18), and the glory of the Lord departure from Israel (4:21).

In addition, the early chapters of 1 Samuel relate the blessings and protection of the Lord that came when His people renewed their obedience to the covenant. From his youth, Samuel paid attention to and listened to the Lord (3:4). Later he enjoined all Israel to pay heed to the Lord (7:3). Samuel led Israel to repent of her sins (7:5, 6). The Lord showed Himself faithful to His people, for He fought the Philistines that day "with a great thunder" (7:10). The Philistines fled in fear (7:13). As long as Samuel judged Israel, the Philistines did not invade the land again (7:14, 15).

Israel eventually grew tired of the judges and requested a king (8:5). God had intended for Israel to have a king, but a king of His choosing and in His time. The Lord's perfect plan for Israel was that the king would be a vassal king under His higher rule. The king would lead the people to keep the covenant and its stipulations. In fact, the king was supposed to copy the law himself and keep it near the throne (Deut. 17:18, 19). The king was to be no greater than his subjects; he was not above the law (17:20). The Lord intended for Israel to function as a theocracy.

3. Read Deuteronomy 17:18–20. What benefits were there in having the king make his own copy of the law?

4. What role was the law to play in the king's life?

5. Why would it be so difficult for a king to follow God's instructions regarding the law?

Explanation of a Theocracy

The word "theocracy" is a theological word. It means "God-ruled." God desired to exercise His rule directly at first, and then indirectly later through a king.

God gave the people a king in response to their request to be like the other nations. God gave Saul to Israel as her first king. King Saul failed because he chose to rebel against the Lord's theocratic rule (1 Sam. 15:23). Samuel had instructed the people to serve the Lord, to obey His voice, and not to "rebel against the commandment of the LORD" so that both the people and the new king would experience the Lord's blessings (12:14, 15).

When the theocracy worked as God intended, He was the ultimate ruler, the Great King. He exercised ultimate rule over Israel's judges and, later, over the kings. The judges and kings evidenced loyalty, allegiance, and obedience to God, since they were His vassals in the treaty partnership.

God explained the stipulations of His rule in the Sinaitic and Deuteronomic Covenants. The Sinaitic Covenant explained what God expected of His people as His special treaty partners. The Deuteronomic Covenant explained what God expected of His people as tenants on His land.

In the theocracy, God wished to reveal Himself to His people through the rulers, but when the rulers failed to obey God, God's revelation was diminished. Therefore, God sent His prophets to warn the kings and the people. God also wished to rescue His people through the rulers, but when they disobeyed Him, He could not bless their military actions. When they did obey, victory was assured.

6. How is a king's role different in a theocracy than in an absolute monarchy?

7. How should these differences have impacted Israel's kings?

In the theocracy God divinely enabled His earthly vassals to rule His people. This divine enabling took the form of a special theocratic anointing by the Holy Spirit. It was a conditional, specialized enabling for rule within the theocracy.

The theocratic anointing occurred throughout the Old Testament theocracy. The Spirit enabled people such as Joshua (Num. 27:18, 20, 23) and the judges to rule (Judg. 3:10; 6:34).

Saul

Saul's character and selection before his coronation foreshadowed his reign. Saul was looking for his father's wandering donkeys when he was first anointed and selected as king. However, Saul grew frustrated and was ready to quit his father's assignment (1 Sam. 9:3–5). The account goes on to reveal that Saul was ignorant of Samuel's ministry (9:18, 19).

As king, God gave Saul the job of leading the people of Israel, who had wandered from God like the wandering donkeys (cf. Isa. 1:3). Saul grew weary of following his Heavenly Father's directives just like he grew weary of his earthly father's directive. And Saul's ignorance of Samuel foreshadowed his eventual disregard for Samuel.

The Lord selected Saul as king because of the people's cry (1 Sam. 9:16). Saul's character and reputation, as well as those who knew him, would not have associated him with the prophets: "Is Saul also among the prophets?" they asked (10:11). The Lord chose Saul, but it is also true that the people chose a king. God gave them the king they desired—a king like those of the nations around them (see 12:13). In the past, God had raised up leaders to deliver the people from their enemies (12:8, 11). At this point, the people wanted a king instead of God, Who was their king (12:12).

8. Why do you think God sometimes gives people what they desire even when it is wrong?

Saul embarked on his reign, being empowered by the Holy Spirit, by defeating Nahash, the king of the Ammonites (1 Sam. 11:1, 6, 7, 11). From that day forward, Saul fought continually (14:47, 52).

Saul's reign was plagued by disobedience. Early in his reign, he disobeyed God by making an unlawful sacrifice to the Lord. Saul justified his actions instead of confessing his sin. The Lord rejected him as king as a result (13:9, 11–14).

Later Saul made his army make a rash vow (14:24, 28, 29). Saul then irrationally wanted to kill his son Jonathan for breaking the vow, even though Jonathan had not consented to it. The people rescued Jonathan from Saul (14:44, 45).

Furthermore, Saul only partially obeyed the Lord by not utterly destroying the Amalekites (15:9–11; 28:18). He came up with several excuses and requests but no confession (15:13–25). Samuel reiterated that God had rejected him for rejecting the word of the LORD (15:26–29).

Saul's final sin, witchcraft at Endor, was the ultimate result of his rebellion against God (15:23; cf. 28:7).

As a king, Saul was fearful (15:24; 17:11; 28:19), paranoid (22:7, 8), and irrational in his rage (20:30–34).

David

The book of 1 Samuel contrasts David's selection and character with Saul's selection and character. First, David was tending his father's sheep in obedience when he was called for his anointing (16:11, 12); Saul was looking for his father's wandering donkeys when he was first anointed as king (9:3, 4).

Second, David was faithful in his shepherding and obedient to his father (16:19; 17:15, 34); Saul was ready to quit his father's assignment (9:5).

Third, David's reputation was one of godliness, prudence, and valor (16:18); Saul's character and reputation led people to ask, "Is Saul also among the prophets?" (10:11).

Fourth, God chose David because he was a man after God's own heart (13:14; 16:1); the people chose Saul because he was like the kings of other nations (12:13).

The summary statement regarding David's selection as the king of Israel appears in Psalm 78:70–72.

9. Read Psalm 78:70–72. How did David's job as a shepherd prepare him to be an effective theocratic king?

God chose David from the "sheepfolds" so that he might shepherd His people Israel. David took care of God's people "according to the integrity of his heart; and guided them by the skillfulness of his hands" (78:72). David's own father and brother saw him only as a shepherd (1 Sam. 16:11; 17:28), but in the pastures of Judah God prepared David for his place in the theocracy (17:33–37).

David's reign is divided into a period of expansion (2 Sam. 2—10) and a time of troubles (2 Sam. 11—24; 1 Kings 1—2:10). David's period of expansion began at Hebron, where he ruled over only Judah. Then he moved his capital city to Jerusalem, where he ruled over all of Israel. David defeated Israel's enemies on every side (2 Sam. 8; 11), and he eventually moved the ark of the covenant to Jerusalem (2 Sam. 6).

David's years of trouble began when he committed adultery with Bathsheba and had her husband, Uriah, killed (11:4, 15). Amnon, David's son, later committed incest with his half-sister, Tamar (chap. 13). David's son Absalom eventually revolted against David (chaps. 14—17). Then Israel rebelled again (19:40—20:22). Finally, the people endured a famine (21:1–14), a plague (chap. 24), and uncertainty during the period of Solomon's accession (1 Kings 1).

10. How does God's choice of David, an imperfect man, encourage your perspective on serving God?

The Davidic Covenant

The Lord had blessed David's reign so that Israel could finally be settled and secure in the Promised Land (2 Sam. 7:9, 10). Unlike the "beforetime" days of the judges when Israel was oppressed, God granted Israel rest in the days of David (7:10b, 11).

After rehearsing God's past dealings with David, God made promises to David through Nathan the prophet. God said He would build a dynasty ("house") for David rather than having David build a house for God (7:11).

Following this general covenant promise of a royal dynasty, God made five specific promises to David (2 Sam. 7:12–16). (1) David would have a son, Solomon, who would succeed him. (2) Solomon would build a house for the Lord. (3) God would establish Solomon's throne and kingdom. (4) God would maintain a special relationship and covenant faithfulness with this son even though the son's sins would bring divine chastening. (7:14b, 15). (5) God would establish David's dynasty ("house"), dominion ("kingdom"), and the right of his descendents to rule ("throne") forever and ever.

The final covenant promise finds ultimate fulfillment in our Lord Jesus Christ. Although Christ does not now reign on David's throne in Jerusalem, He will one day return to the earth to establish His worldwide kingdom from Israel (Matt. 19:28).

11. Read Psalm 89:19–37. How clear is the fact that the future reign of David's seed, Christ, is unconditional and permanent?

12. How should the sure promise of the reign of Christ in the millennium affect your life?

Solomon

Solomon, David's second son by Bathsheba, reigned in David's place (1 Kings 2:12). After securing his throne (2:13–46), he asked for wisdom from God (3:7–14). "Solomon's wisdom excelled the wisdom of all the children of the east country, and all the wisdom of Egypt" (4:30; cf. 10:1–13). Solomon was also fabulously wealthy (10:14–29). His crowning achievement was building the temple (5:1—6:38; 2 Chron. 2:1—5:1).

Solomon's failures stemmed from his direct disobedience to the Deuteronomic Covenant (Deut. 17:16, 17). According to the covenant, the king (1) was not to "multiply horses to himself," (2) "nor cause the people to return to Egypt," (3) nor was he to "multiply wives to himself," (4) nor was he to "greatly multiply to himself silver and gold."

Solomon disobeyed God on all four points. (1) He multiplied horses (1 Kings 10:26). (2) He sent his merchants to Egypt for chariots, horses, and linen (10:27–29). (3) He had seven hundred wives and three hundred concubines (11:1, 3; cf. Exod. 34:13–16; Deut. 7:3, 4). (4) He "made silver and gold at Jerusalem as plenteous as stones" (2 Chron. 1:15). Because Solomon did not keep the covenant, God promised to give the kingdom to one of his servants, Jeroboam, in the days of his son, Rehoboam (1 Kings 11:11, 26, 35, 40, 43).

Solomon's rise and fall affords a sobering reminder to believers that obedience ought to be a lifelong endeavor. The account also reminds believers of God's mercy and faithfulness, for He left one tribe to David's dynasty because of David's obedience and because of God's promise in the Davidic Covenant (11:36, 38, 39).

13. What does it take to obey God your King for your entire life?

14. What warnings and lessons can you glean from Solomon's life regarding obedience to God?

Making It Personal

15. If sometime in the future others were to read about this present portion of your life, would they be reading about your general obedience to God? Or would they be reading of your failure through disobedience to God?

16. What will you do this week to increase your obedience to God? Who could you share your commitment with?

In countries ruled by a monarch, the monarch's image appears on currency; the image of the crown or royal seal is found on all official documents. God is a spirit and therefore we cannot put His image on things. However our lives are to be marked by godliness.

17. Why is it important to reflect God through the way you live?

18. What are some attitudes and actions that would reflect God to others watching your life?

19. Memorize Psalm 89:34–36.

Revelation and Redemption in the Divided Kingdom

God is just in His dealings, faithful to His covenants, and sovereign over history.

1 Kings 12; 17—22; 2 Chron. 17—20

"And [Jehoshaphat] said, O Lord God of our fathers, art not thou God in heaven? and rulest not thou over all the kingdoms of the heathen? and in thine hand is there not power and might, so that none is able to withstand thee?" (2 Chronicles 20:6).

For about the past 100 years, the famous *Farmers' Almanac* has been providing annual weather forecasts. And even though the almanac's accuracy rates are really no better than chance, people take their predictions seriously. Around 4 million people buy the annual periodical so they can speak like an expert and tell everyone what the next season's weather will be like. "The *Farmers' Almanac* says . . ."

Getting Started

1. What are examples of people or professions that prognosticate?

2. What makes these people either reliable or unreliable?

This lesson highlights God's sovereignty demonstrated through His prophets. Unlike so-called modern day prophets, true Biblical prophets speak with clear accuracy.

Searching the Scriptures

The history of Israel is largely recorded in the books of Kings and Chronicles. Both have different emphases and perspectives.

The books of 1 and 2 Samuel and 1 and 2 Kings view the history of Israel and Judah in terms of the Deuteronomic Covenant. The books of 1 and 2 Chronicles view the history of Judah in terms of the priestly legislation in the Sinaitic Covenant.

The books of Samuel and Kings provide the perspective of the prophets, including Elijah and Elisha. The books record the many times that the prophets warned that disobedience would result in expulsion from the Promised Land.

Chronicles provides the priestly perspective and mainly assesses the kings of Judah since the temple resided in Jerusalem, Judah's capital.

Survey of the Divided Kingdom

After the death of Solomon, his son Rehoboam took the throne (2 Sam. 11:43). The people of Israel complained about the heavy taxation under Solomon's reign. Rehoboam pledged to rethink the taxation policies. Three days later he met with the leaders of Israel. Rehoboam rejected the advice of the older men and followed the advice of the younger men. He treated the people roughly and promised even higher taxes.

The people of the northern ten tribes, Israel, revolted and made Jeroboam their king (1 Kings 12:1–24). The Lord told Solomon this would happen (11:29–32).

Jeroboam did not want his people going down to Jerusalem to worship for fear they would revert their loyalty to the Davidic dynasty

(12:25–33). So he set a golden calf in Bethel, just eleven miles north of Jerusalem, and another one at Dan in the far north region of Israel. He enlisted non-Levites to serve as priests at these idolatrous shrines (12:31; 13:33, 34).

Jeroboam did not trust the Lord to establish his authority over the northern tribes. Therefore, the Lord sent one of His prophets to Jeroboam with a stern denouncement and a detailed prediction that named Josiah, a future king of Judah, three hundred years before Josiah ascended to the throne (13:1–5).

3. Why might people consider worshiping God a threat to their power or authority?

4. Name a godly leader who leads while affirming God's ultimate rule.

Over the years, twenty different kings ruled the Northern Kingdom. These kings came from three major dynasties plus several short-lived ones. The three major dynasties were those established by Jeroboam I, Omri, and Jehu. The most notorious king from Omri's dynasty was Ahab (1 Kings 16:29—22:40).

Not one of Israel's kings was a good king. The final king of Israel was Hoshea (2 Kings 17). His reign ended when the Assyrians destroyed the capital city of Samaria and deported the people of Israel from their land in 722 BC.

Twenty different kings ruled the Southern Kingdom. Asa, Jehoshaphat, Joash, Uzziah/Azariah, Jotham, Hezekiah, and Josiah were good kings. Uzziah was a leader of a renaissance. Hezekiah was a friend of the prophet Isaiah. Manasseh was the most wicked and longest reigning king. And Josiah was the boy king and probably the godliest. The Scriptures call these kings good despite some of their recorded sins and shortfalls.

The final king of Judah was Zedekiah (2 Kings 24:18—25:21; 2 Chron. 36:11–21). His reign ended in 586 BC, when Nebuchadnezzar, king of Babylon, destroyed Jerusalem and deported many of the people to Babylon.

5. What lessons about God's sovereignty can we learn from considering a survey of the kings in the Divided Kingdom?

Since this study merely surveys the Old Testament story, this lesson will focus on only two kings, one from Israel and one from Judah. These two kings are representative in many ways of the other kings. They ruled at about the same time and cooperated in several endeavors. Their reigns are a sharp contrast of one another.

Ahab in Israel

Ahab "did more to provoke the LORD God of Israel to anger than all the kings of Israel that were before him" (1 Kings 16:30, 33). Later, 1 Kings records that "there was none like unto Ahab, which did sell himself to work wickedness in the sight of the LORD, whom Jezebel his wife stirred up" (21:25). Ahab followed the sinful ways of Jeroboam I, but he went beyond the wickedness of Jeroboam by aggressively promoting Baalism.

6. What does calling a person a "Jezebel" say about that person's character?

Ahab's wife, the wicked queen Jezebel, the Sidonian (16:31), sponsored Baalism throughout Israel. Hundreds of false prophets lived on her royal payroll (18:19). Baalism was an exceedingly immoral form of idolatry because of its fertility rites. It was worse than the idolatrous system instituted by Jeroboam I.

Ahab endorsed Jezebel's religious program. When he coveted Naboth's vineyard and wanted to buy it, Naboth refused because it was his family inheritance according to the stipulations of the covenant (1 Kings 21:1–3; Lev. 25:23–28; Num. 36:7, 8). Ahab pouted at the response, so Jezebel promised her husband that she would acquire the vineyard for him (1 Kings 21:4–7).

Jezebel decided that if Naboth wished to live by the covenant, then he would die by the covenant. She sent letters throughout Jezreel, Naboth's hometown, in Ahab's name. The letters contained false charges corroborated by two false witnesses (1 Kings 21:8–11; Deut. 17:6).

After fasting, the elders of the city held a mock trial. They found Naboth guilty of blaspheming God and the king (1 Kings 21:12, 13a; Lev. 24:14–16). The people stoned Naboth and his sons to death (1 Kings 21:13b; 2 Kings 9:26). Jezebel brought Naboth's family line to an end. So she told Ahab to arise and take possession of the vineyard (1 Kings 21:14–16).

Ahab's sin was so egregious that God promised through Elijah that Ahab's dogs would lick up his blood in the same spot where they had licked up Naboth's blood (21:19). The prophesy, of course, came true (22:37, 38).

7. Read 1 Kings 22:1–40. How is God's sovereignty demonstrated in the account of Ahab's death?

8. What lessons about God's sovereignty can we glean from this account?

Micaiah, the prophet, predicted Ahab's death at the battle of Ramoth Gilead (22:14–18). Ahab believed the prophecy enough to disguise himself and to ask Jehoshaphat to ride into battle as a king (22:30). Nevertheless, the Lord's words are always accomplished.

A Syrian archer released an arrow at random. It hit Ahab in the

joints of his armor (22:34). The wound was fatal; Ahab died that evening (22:35). Ahab's men took his body in his chariot back to Samaria.
When they washed the chariot, the dogs licked up Ahab's blood (22:37,
38). God's justice is clearly shown in Ahab's demise.

Jehoshaphat in Judah

Jehoshaphat was a godly king who "walked in the first ways of
his father David, and sought not unto Baalim" (2 Chron.17:3). Jehoshaphat "sought to the LORD God of his father [Asa], and walked in his
commandments, and not after the doings of Israel" (17:4). For the most
part, Jehoshaphat, whose "heart was lifted up in the ways of the LORD,"
removed the idolatrous high places in Judah (17:6; 19:3). Jehoshaphat
sent princes and Levites throughout his country to teach the people the
law of the Lord (17:7–9). He also set judges in the fortified cities of Judah to render judgments according to the laws of God (19:5, 10).

9. Read 2 Chronicles 20:1–30. How is God's sovereignty showcased
in the account of Jehoshaphat's defeat of the multitude?

10. What lessons about God's sovereignty can we glean from Jehoshaphat's life?

Jehoshaphat received tribute from the Philistines and Arabians
(17:11). He also defeated the coalition of Moabites, Ammonites, and
Edomites (20:1, 10).

More properly, the Lord defeated the coalition for Jehoshaphat. The
king prayed to the Lord and asked God to show Himself faithful to the
covenants (Abrahamic in 2 Chron. 20:7; Deuteronomic in 20:8–12).

God heard the prayer and fought for Israel (2 Chron. 20:17). Judah
sent singers into battle, and the coalition destroyed itself (20:21–23).
The people of Judah carried away great plunder (20:24, 25). The battle

reinforced God's faithfulness to His covenant promises. It also revealed how God was eager to redeem His people from their enemies.

11. Read 2 Chronicles 20:7–12. What does Jehoshaphat's prayer reveal about his beliefs about God at that time?

Unfortunately, Jehoshaphat's faith in God was not always strong. He wavered by making alliances with kings of Israel (2 Chron. 18:1–3; 20:35). He allied himself with Ahab in the military campaign at Ramoth Gilead where he almost got himself killed (18:28, 31). When Jehoshaphat returned to Judah from Ramoth Gilead, the prophet Jehu met him with a message from God: "Shouldest thou help the ungodly, and love them that hate the LORD?" (19:2).

Later Jehoshaphat allied himself with Ahaziah in the shipping venture at Ezion Geber (20:35, 36). Eliezer the prophet condemned Jehoshaphat for this unholy alliance.

12. Read 2 Chronicles 20:35–37. What did God sovereignly do as a result of Jehoshaphat's attempt at economic gain through an unholy alliance?

Doubtless, the worst alliance decision Jehoshaphat made was marrying his son, Jehoram or Joram, to Athaliah, daughter of Ahab and granddaughter of Omri (2 Kings 8:16–18, 26).

13. Why would Jehoshaphat have his son marry Ahab's daughter? What would such an action suggest about Jehoshaphat's belief in God?

The marriage between Jehoram and Athaliah opened Judah to Baalism following Jehoshaphat's death. The alliance nearly resulted in the extinction of the Davidic line (8:27; 11:1, 2).

The Prophets' Messages

The prophets played an important role in the history of the kingdoms of Israel and Judah. Determining the function of the Old Testament prophet begins with an analysis of the words "seer" and "prophet." That the term "seer" comes from two roots that mean "to see" (1 Sam. 9:9) and "to envision" (Amos 7:12). The word "seer," then, emphasized the receptive aspect of the prophetic office.

The term "prophet" emphasized the revelatory aspect of the prophetic office. The prophet revealed the message that he had received from God. Often, the messages had a futuristic sense to them; hence, the prophet often made predictions.

14. Read Deuteronomy 18:20–22. How were people to decipher whether a prophet was truly from God?

15. What is the connection between prophets and the sovereignty of God?

Fundamentally, of course, the prophetic function was to convey the "word of the Lord." Their messages came from the Lord, and their messages invariably accomplished their desired result.

The prophets occasionally communicated by means of symbolic acts. For example, Isaiah walked naked (Isa. 20:1–6), Jeremiah used a yoke (Jer. 27; 28), Ahijah tore a garment (1 Kings 11:30), and Ezekiel employed symbolic acts (Ezek. 4; 5).

In addition to making numerous predictions, the prophets also spoke to the moral issues of their day. They functioned as God's divinely appointed moral preachers and teachers of the covenant stipulations, especially of the Deuteronomic Covenant. They constantly threatened the people that they would be deported from the land because of their disobedience (Jer. 16:10–13). The prophets sounded warnings against the dangers of religious apostasy (Jer. 25:4–7) and against mere religious formalism (1 Sam. 15:22; Micah 6:6–8). In this regard they sometimes confronted kings (1 Kings 13:4; 17:1; Jer. 22:24–30).

16. Why do you think much of the prophets' ministries, as recorded in the Bible, were focused on interacting with the kings?

The prophets occasionally anointed the kings to signify that royal rule was a bequest from God.

Elijah and Elisha exemplified prophetic ideals and illustrated the function of the prophetic office in the theocracy. Elijah served during and after the years of kings Ahab and Jehoshaphat. Elisha picked up where Elijah left off. These men fought idolatry, performed miracles, and trained future prophets.

Prophets' View of History

The Old Testament story is inextricably tied to the work of the prophets. Actually, the prophets told the Old Testament story (Heb. 1:1) of revelation and redemption. Their proclamations revealed God and His will to the people.

The prophets gave prophetic interpretations of the great events of Israelite history. They were aware of God's providence in all events of history, whereby He was guiding all to one central purpose: the establishment of His kingdom upon the earth, the final and full realization of the theocracy (Isa. 45:22, 23; Zech. 14:9).

Since God controls history, He can control the future and can guarantee the fulfillment of the prophets' predictions (Isa. 46:9, 10; Amos 3:7). The prophets revealed the holiness and justice of God, but they also revealed the faithfulness and sovereignty of God.

17. How should the prophets' confidence in God to bring prophecy to pass affect our confidence in God?

Making It Personal

God's sovereignty was demonstrated in a variety ways in the time period of the Divided Kingdom. God is still sovereign.

18. How have you seen God's sovereign hand at work in your past?

19. Who has God providentially brought into your life to accomplish His purposes?

20. Spend time praising God for your experiences of God's sovereignty.

21. What circumstances in your life challenge your belief in the sovereignty of God?

22. Pray about the areas of your life that threaten your trust in God's sovereignty. Pray your faith would be strengthened and you would know God's grace.

23. Memorize 2 Chronicles 20:6.

Revelation and Redemption after the Kingdom

God tempers His justice with His mercy and provides hope.

2 Kings 24; 25; Ezra; Nehemiah; Esther; Lam. 4; Habakkuk

"And Shechaniah . . . said unto Ezra, We have trespassed against our God, and have taken strange wives of the people of the land: yet now there is hope in Israel concerning this thing" (Ezra 10:2).

Children who do not have a healthy respect for their parents and other authorities in their lives will probably not be "good kids." They probably won't be very happy either! Trying to usurp authorities and control one's life ironically leaves a person dissatisfied and empty. The Israelites experienced this truth over and over again.

Getting Started

1. Would you consider God's punishment of sin frightening? Why?

2. How might God's punishment of sin be a comfort?

In the lesson we see God's justice and mercy displayed. God's justice should be a comfort to believers as we are reminded that God does deal with evil. Believers need not be scared of God, but they should have a healthy respect for His discipline. He has promised to discipline His children.

Searching the Scriptures

3. Given the conditional nature of the Sinaitic Covenant, what should God's people have expected God to do in the face of their continual disobedience during the time of the divided kingdom?

In this lesson we will see that God did indeed bring judgment on His people as they deserved, yet He promised hope at the same time.

Daniel: First Deportation

After defeating the Egyptians and Assyrians at Carchemish in May/ June 605 BC, Nebuchadnezzar chased the Egyptians as they retreated southward to Egypt (2 Kings 24:7). Nebuchadnezzar marched south through Syria and Israel and entered Judah. Nebuchadnezzar went up to Jerusalem and obligated Judah's king, Jehoiakim, to serve him (24:1). At that time, Nebuchadnezzar took treasures from the temple and children from the palace (Dan. 1:1–4). Nebuchadnezzar took the treasures into the temple of his god and took the youth to Babylon for training. Daniel and his three friends were among these first deportees.

4. Read Daniel 1:1, 2. What was God's role and what was Nebuchadnezzar's role in Judah's initial defeat?

Ezekiel: Second Deportation

After Jehoiakim died, his son, Jehoiachin, reigned in his place (2 Kings 24:6). Very early in his short three-month reign, Jehoiachin rebelled against Nebuchadnezzar. In response, Nebuchadnezzar besieged the city of Jerusalem for a second time (24:11). The city fell on March 16, 597 BC (24:12). Nebuchadnezzar looted even more treasures from the temple (24:13). He also deported ten thousand of the leading citizens, including Ezekiel and King Jehoiachin (24:14). Nebuchadnezzar enthroned Jehoiachin's uncle as king and changed his name to Zedekiah (2 Kings 24:17).

Zedekiah: Third Deportation

Eventually, Zedekiah rebelled against Nebuchadnezzar (2 Kings 24:20). So Nebuchadnezzar came to Jerusalem and set up a siege for the third time. The siege lasted until the city fell in 586 BC (25:8). Before the city fell, Zedekiah and his small army tried to escape the siege. The Babylonians pursued them to Jericho and defeated them there (25:4, 5).

Nebuchadnezzar executed Zedekiah's sons before his eyes, blinded Zedekiah, and deported him to Babylon (25:7). The punishment fulfilled two prophecies: (1) Jeremiah had predicted that Zedekiah would speak with Nebuchadnezzar face to face (Jer. 32:4; 34:3) and (2) Ezekiel had predicted that Zedekiah would not *see* Babylon (Ezek. 12:13).

The Babylonians broke down Jerusalem's walls and burned the temple and palace (2 Kings 25:9, 10). They deported 832 adult males (Jer. 52:29) but left the poor behind to tend the fields (Jer. 39:10; 2 Kings 25:12). The Babylonians carted off the remaining treasures of the temple (2 Kings 25:13–17).

5. Do you think the consequences of sin are more prevalent today or during the time of Israel's deportation by the Babylonians? Why?

6. Read Lamentations 4:8–16. How do these verses challenge or confirm your opinion?

The terrible circumstances in Jerusalem happened because God loosed His righteous fury against sinful Jerusalem (Lam. 4:11). The false prophets, the sinful priests, and the people bent on violence unleashed the anger of the Lord (4:13–16; cf. 2 Kings 24:14). During the years of sinful rebellion, God had compassion on His people and on their houses. He sent His prophets to warn His people, to call them to repentance. But the people mistreated God's messengers "until the wrath of the LORD arose against his people, till there was no remedy" (2 Chron. 36:15, 16). God revealed His compassion both by sending the prophets and by promising the eventual reversal of the captivity after seventy years (Lam. 4:22).

The sieges, deportations, and judgments of God were tempered by His love and mercy. God judged on the basis of the Deuteronomic Covenant, but He pardoned on the basis of the Abrahamic Covenant. The Babylonians deported the people, but the Persians, who in turn defeated the Babylonians, would let the Jews return (2 Chron. 36:20).

Living on the land was conditional, but possessing the land was unconditional.

7. Why might people fail to notice God's merciful acts that often accompany judgment?

Israel in Exile—Punishment

The exile came as punishment for covenant disobedience. The seventy years in Babylonian exile provided the Promised Land with rest from all the violent sins of the people. The years also purged the Israelites of their tendency toward pagan polytheism.

The prophet Habakkuk wrote a short treatise that deals with sinful Judah and the Babylonian invasions.

The Lord explained to Habakkuk that the Babylonians would punish Israel for her sins. Habakkuk looked at the violence and iniquity of the people of Judah and asked God if He would allow sinners to go unpunished and if He would save the righteous (Hab.1:2, 4). The Lord answered that He would raise up the Chaldeans (Babylonians) to punish His people in Judah (1:6). Habakkuk then asked a follow-up question: Why would God use the Babylonians to punish Judah, since the Babylonians were more sinful than God's people (1:12, 13)? The Lord answered that He would eventually destroy the Babylonians (2:8).

8. Read Habakkuk 3. Note some of the attributes of God extolled in this prayer.

9. How does Habakkuk's prayer teach you to praise God's justice, wrath, and power?

Although the Babylonians would devastate the Promised Land (3:17), the prophet would rejoice in the Lord. He exclaimed: "I will joy in the God of my salvation" (3:18). No matter the circumstances, Habakkuk would find strength in the Lord (3:19).

Habakkuk's prophecy illustrates the close connection between history and theology in the Old Testament. The Old Testament is a story of God's attributes in action. As God revealed Himself to the Jews, He drew the exiles back to Himself.

10. What theological truths have you been reminded of by considering the historical realities of the exile?

Israel in Exile—Protection

While the Jews lived in Babylon, the Lord protected them from their enemies. The accounts of the three Hebrew young men in the fiery furnace (Dan. 3) and of Daniel in the lion's den (Dan. 6) exemplify the

Lord's protection of His people. The Lord kept His people for the duration of the exile (Dan. 1:21).

The most extensive story of God's protection during the dispersion appears in the fascinating account of Esther. Esther became the chief queen in the Persian Empire without revealing her Jewish identity or familial relationship to Mordecai (Esther 2:17). Haman, the prime minister (3:1), hated Mordecai and all the Jews (3:6). Therefore, Haman asked King Ahasuerus to issue an edict throughout the empire to kill all the Jews (3:10, 13, 14).

Mordecai appealed to Esther to use her position to influence Ahasuerus into issuing a reprieve (4:13, 14). Esther risked her life by going uninvited before the king and inviting him and Haman to a private banquet at her residence (4:11; 5:1–4). At the banquet, Esther asked the two to come to a second banquet (5:8).

That night, the king could not sleep, so he asked that the royal record be read to him (6:1). His servants read the account of how Mordecai had uncovered an assassination plot against the king (6:2). The king asked what reward had been given to Mordecai. The servants answered that none had been given (6:3). Just then Haman entered the court to ask permission to hang Mordecai before the assigned holocaust date (6:4). Before answering, Ahasuerus asked Haman a question: "What shall be done unto the man whom the king delighteth to honour" (6:6)? Haman felt that the king must have been referring to him, so he came up with a long list of honors (6:6b–9). Ahasuerus commanded Haman to do these very things for Mordecai (6:10)!

That evening at Esther's banquet, the queen told her husband how Haman had plotted to hang Mordecai and to kill all the Jews, her people (7:3–5). The king commanded that Haman be hanged on the gallows he had prepared for Mordecai (7:9, 10). The king also issued a second edict allowing the Jews to defend themselves (8:11). The Lord placed fear in all the Jews' enemies so that the Jews were victorious (9:5, 6, 16).

Ahasuerus made Mordecai his new prime minister (9:4) and ordered Haman's ten sons to be hanged (9:14).

The account of Esther cleverly reveals God's sovereignty over the affairs of men. God is not mentioned by name in the book. Men make their plans and plots, but the God they disregard always accomplishes His will.

11. How might God's providential work demonstrated in the book of Esther encourage believers today?

Return—Zerrubabel and the Remnant

In the first year that Cyrus the Persian conquered the Babylonian Empire, Cyrus commanded the returning Jews to rebuild the temple in Jerusalem (Ezra 1:1–6). Cyrus even returned the original temple treasures that he had taken from the Babylonians (1:7–11).

A total of 49,897 of the exiled Jews returned to Judea in 536 BC (Ezra 2:64, 65). The people rebuilt the altar in Jerusalem and started to rebuild the temple in 536 BC. The effort was short-lived; they stopped the next year (3:3, 10; 4:24).

For fifteen years the temple project languished. Then in 520 BC, Haggai and Zechariah exhorted the leaders and the people to complete the temple (Ezra 5:1, 2). The people completed it in 515 BC and celebrated the Passover (6:15, 19–22).

12. Read Haggai 2:1–9. Which aspect of the Sinaitic Covenant did Haggai appeal to in his exhortation of Zerrubabel in verse 5 (cf. Exodus 29:45, 46)?

13. Why would God's presence with the Jews be so important to them?

After the builders had laid the foundation of the temple, many of the older people lamented because the new temple was so much smaller than the old one (Ezra 3:12, 13). The older generation responded similarly when the people renewed their rebuilding efforts in the days of Haggai (Hag. 2:3). Haggai, himself a member of the older generation, encouraged Zerrubabel to be strong in the Lord (2:4). To encourage the people, Haggai invoked the promise of God's presence that God had made with Israel in the Sinaitic Covenant (Hag. 2:5; cf. Exod. 29:45, 46).

Return—Ezra and the Temple

Ezra, the priest, and 1,496 people with him, returned to Jerusalem from captivity in 458 BC (Ezra 7; 8). Ezra found the Jewish community intermarrying with pagan people (9:1, 2). Ezra was so distraught that he pulled his own hair out (9:3). He called the people to repentance and covenanted with them that they would put away their pagan wives (10:3).

What concerned Ezra was that the Lord had punished Israel with deportation for her many sins. The people were again slipping into sin (9:6–10). The people agreed with Ezra that they needed to live separated, holy lives unto God (10:11, 12). Ezra's ministry highlights God's expectation of holy living.

14. Read Ezra 9:1, 2. Why did Israel fall into sin even though the ruins of Jerusalem's destruction still lay all around them?

15. Read Ezra 10:1–5. Why was there still hope in Israel?

Return—Nehemiah and the Walls

Nehemiah, a courtier in the Persian palace at Shushan, returned to rebuild the walls of Jerusalem in 444 BC (Neh. 1:1; 2:1, 5). Soon after he arrived in Jerusalem, Nehemiah began directing in the wall-rebuilding project (2:18). He delegated sections of the wall to various family units, making sure that people would build those sections of the wall nearest to their own homes (Neh. 3).

The pagans who lived near Jerusalem tried to discourage and

threaten the workers (4:2, 3, 8). Nevertheless, the work progressed both because "the people had a mind to work" and because all the workers armed themselves and took turns guarding the city (4:6, 16, 17, 21).

The people worked so hard that they did not even take off their clothes except to wash them (4:23). Their hard work made the project progress rapidly until only the gates remained (6:1).

Sanballat and Tobiah, enemies of the Jews, sent for Nehemiah to entrap him (6:1, 2). Nehemiah refused to talk with them because the work was a great work (6:3).

Nehemiah exhibited persistence and focus. The people finished the wall in only fifty-two days because the "work was wrought of our God" (6:15, 16).

One week after the completion of the wall, Ezra and other Levites read the law of God to the people (8:2–4, 7, 8). The people wept because of their sins. The Levites stilled them (8:9, 11). On the next day, the people observed the Feast of Tabernacles. There was great gladness in the city during the weeklong feast as the people heard God's Word read and explained (8:13–18).

Two days after the festival, the people acknowledged their sin still further (9:1). In response to their renewed sensitivity to sin, the Levites reminded the people of their national history.

16. Read Nehemiah 9:7–15. What covenants did the Levites reference in these verses?

17. Why were the covenants still valid centuries after God made them?

The Levites taught that God is merciful, gracious, mighty, awesome, faithful, and just (Neh. 9:31–33). The Levites also led the people to renew their covenant commitment (9:38).

Near the end of Nehemiah's ministry, the sin of pagan and Jewish marriages occurred again. Nehemiah, unlike Ezra, did not pull out his own hair; Nehemiah pulled out the offenders' hair (13:23–25). He exhorted the people to consider Solomon who, though he was a great king, was influenced to sin by his wives (13:26).

Making It Personal

The Jews were never without hope. God was faithful to them and remained with them in their darkest hours.

18. What reasons do you have for hope in God?

19. What reasons for hope in God will you focus on this week?

20. Memorize Ezra 10:2.

Lesson 10

Israel Responds to God's Revelation and Redemption

God's revelation and redemption should result in worship and thanksgiving.

Exod. 15; Deut. 32; Judg. 5; 2 Sam. 22; Ps. 14; 19; 22; 51; 90; 119

"Praise ye the LORD: for it is good to sing praises unto our God; for it is pleasant; and praise is comely" (Ps. 147:1).

R ock-a-bye baby on the treetop." Most likely the words "when the wind blows, the cradle will rock" just went through your head. Rhymes have a way of sticking with us even when they are completely nonsensical. It doesn't makes sense, after all, to sing a lullaby about a baby falling out of a tree!

Getting Started

1. What rhymes are forever imbedded in your memory?

2. What makes those rhymes hard to forget?

Hebrew poetry aims for parallelism rather than rhyme. In parallelism the second phrase in each couplet states the same thing in different words (synonymous parallelism), the opposite thing (antithetical parallelism), or an additional thing (synthetic parallelism). While parallelism may not make psalms easier to remember, it does fill psalms with powerful meaning.

Searching the Scriptures

Song of Moses and Miriam

The Old Testament is an account of God's self-revelation as well as His acts of redemption. At times, the people of Israel responded to God's revelation and redemption with songs of thanksgiving and praise. One such hymn appears in Exodus 15. Moses and the children of Israel sang this song after the Lord delivered them through the Red Sea.

3. Read Exodus 15:2. Why was the personal nature of this verse so appropriate for each of the children of Israel to sing?

The song exalts God because He is a warrior Who "dashed in pieces the enemy" (15:3, 6), controls the wind and the sea (15:5, 8, 10), and is "glorious in holiness" (15:11).

The psalm predicted fear and dread would fall on Canaan and that the Lord would bring His people into their promised possession (15:14–17).

4. What are some songs you enjoy that focus on God's redemption?

Song of Moses

Before Moses died, he taught a song to Israel (Deut. 32). It rehearses the entire history of Israel and is instructional (Deut. 32:46).

5. Read Deuteronomy 32:2. How does Moses' word picture in this verse help communicate the importance of his song's message?

The psalm includes the division of the nations and the selection of Jacob as God's special inheritance (32:8, 9). It then mentions the Lord's special care during the wilderness wanderings right up to the Israelites' entrance into the Transjordanian region (32:12–14).

The song truthfully refers to Israel's rebellions against God (32:15–18). It also describes God's holy anger against Israel, which would allow Israel's enemies to defeat her (32:19–26).

6. Read Deuteronomy 32:15–18. Why was it important for Israel to remember past failures in her relationship with God?

With this song, Moses also taught the people that God would limit the victories of Israel's enemies lest the enemies gloated in their own power (32:27–35). The Lord would judge His people rather than leaving judgment to the nations (32:36–39).

Song of Deborah and Barak

The song of Deborah and Barak in Judges 5 provides some excellent examples of Hebrew poetry. The prose account in chapter 4 is straightforward with the feel of clipped prose. Everything is stated economically. This style contrasts with the poetic account in chapter 5. The poetic song is more repetitive in its phrasing; in places it even has a cadence. The story in the song ends on a dramatic note (5:28–30).

7. Read Judges 5:28–30. What is your response as you read this dramatic scene?

The song ends by asking God to deal with all the enemies of Israel as He had dealt with the enemies of Deborah and Barak (5:31). The "love" expresses covenant faithfulness.

8. Read Judges 5:31. What do Deborah and Barak communicate through the word picture in this final portion of their song?

The song tells a story of God's deliverance, but it also says much about God directly. So it is a more historical song than the song of Moses.

Song of David

King David wrote more psalms than any other person. Many of David's psalms reflect the love of God and the future redemption that would come through the Messiah—David's promised Descendant. Some of David's psalms appear outside the book of Psalms.

Second Samuel 22 records David's personal thanksgiving that the Lord had delivered him from Saul and from all of his enemies (v. 1). The hymn comprises three major sections: (1) praise that the Lord delivered David from his enemies who wanted to kill him (2 Sam. 22:5–20); (2) praise that the Lord rewarded David because he was God's servant (22:21–30); and (3) praise that the Lord protected David to reveal His greatness and power (22:31–46). David likely wrote this song after the Lord made the Davidic Covenant with him (see 22:51).

This song of David involves much personal praise rather than national praise. David bared his soul.

9. Read 2 Samuel 22:2–4, 47. How does David's personal praise of God help *you* praise God personally?

The Book of Psalms

Most of the songs in the Old Testament are in the book of Psalms. "Praises" is the Hebrew title for this collection of songs. The Hebrew verb from which the Hebrew title is derived means "to shout for joy, to rejoice."

David wrote more psalms than anyone else, but others wrote psalms as well. Moses, Asaph, the sons of Korah, Solomon, Heman, and Ethan wrote some of the psalms. All of these men reflected upon the one true God of Israel Who made the heavens and the earth (Ps. 146:5, 6). And each writer lifted his heart to God in praise so that "everything that hath breath [might] praise the LORD" (150:6). The psalms respond to God's revelation and to His great works of redemption.

Responding to God's Work

"The heavens declare the glory of God; and the firmament sheweth his handiwork" (Ps. 19:1). David sang what Moses wrote about God's creation. The stars, sun, moon, and planets show that God deserves honor. The sky tells of what God has done (19:4–6). God has given His Word so that those who read it might know Him and might do His will, but His creation reveals His works so that all might know His creative power (19:3).

God works within His creation and controls it. "He casteth forth his ice like morsels: who can stand before his cold? He sendeth out his word, and melteth them: he causeth his wind to blow, and the waters flow" (147:17, 18). God knows every star by name (19:4). He calls forth rain and feeds the animals (19:8, 9).

Creation must respond to the Creator. Some civilizations have worshiped the creation, but the psalms invoke praise to the Creator (148:3–5).

10. When have you been moved to praise God as you observed His creation?

Responding to God's Word

David began Psalm 19 by pointing to God's creative works and the way that these works reveal His mighty power. David finished Psalm 19 by singing about God's marvelous Word.

God's creative works are great, but the "law of the LORD is perfect" (19:7). God's Word makes one wise, gives joy and enlightenment, and brings purity and righteousness (19:7b–9). It is little wonder, then, that David likened the value of God's Word to gold and the sweetness of His Word to honey (19:10). David referred to the role that God's Word plays in shielding the believer from sin: warning, rewarding, and protecting (19:11–13).

11. Read Psalm 19:10. What word picture would you use to describe the value of God's Word to you?

The writer of Psalm 119 added even more praise to God for His Word. The psalm is structured as an acrostic poem with each section of verses beginning with the next letter in the Hebrew alphabet. Nearly every verse in this hymn praises God for His Word.

The psalm uses various terms to refer to God's Word, including "way," "commandment," "judgment," "testimony," "statute," "precept," "saying," and "law". These terms describe the Word of God, which cleanses, guides, guards, and enriches people (119:9–11, 14).

12. Read Psalm 119:14–16. How have you delighted in and rejoiced in God's Word?

Responding to God's Worth

The psalms not only show how God reveals Himself in His works and in His Word, they also reveal His worth. The psalms repeat, describe, explain, and illustrate time and again the attributes of God.

Moses declared, "LORD, thou hast been our dwelling place in all generations. Before the mountains were brought forth, or ever thou hadst formed the earth and the world, even from everlasting to everlasting, thou art God" (90:1, 2). Time cannot contain God because He is eternal.

The psalms describe God as "holy" (set apart from evil). His dwelling is holy (11:4; 15:1). His name is holy (97:12; 103:1). He's holy (29:2; 30:4).

The psalms also reveal how God shows judgment and love at the same time. "God judgeth the righteous, and God is angry with the wicked every day" (7:11). He is righteous and will judge sin, but He will also have compassion on those who, like David, seek His forgiveness. David cried, "Have mercy upon me, O God, according to thy loving-kindness: according unto the multitude of thy tender mercies blot out my transgressions" (51:1).

God is omnipotent, omniscient, and omnipresent. He is all-powerful, all-knowing, and present everywhere at once: "Great is our Lord, and of great power: his understanding is infinite" (147:5). "Whither shall I go from thy spirit? Or whither shall I flee from thy presence?" (139:7).

13. How might we praise and thank God for His revelation of Himself?

Admitting a Need for Redemption

God gave His Word so that people might understand His plan of redemption. The psalms give an evenhanded assessment of lost humanity. The apostle Paul quoted Psalm 14 when said all have sinned and deserve God's punishment (Ps. 14:1b–3; cf. Rom. 3:10–12).

14. Why is it important to rehearse humanity's depravity so often?

Repeatedly the psalmists requested God's mercy and deliverance. Sometimes the psalmists requested deliverance from calamity or from enemies and sometimes from sin and foolishness (Ps. 107:2).

David asked for God's forgiveness and cleansing (51:1, 2). He admitted his own original sin (51:5). And he expressed belief that God would forgive him for all of his sins (51:7–10). David also exhibited a truly contrite heart, real repentance for his sins (51:16, 17). God does not disappoint the repentant sinner (34:22).

Since the need for redemption is so great and God has met that need, the psalmists encouraged Israel to rejoice in God's redemption (130:7).

15. Read Psalm 117. What would you say to someone who thinks he has no reason to praise God?

16. Why is the everlasting nature of the Lord's truth a reason to praise God?

Acknowledging the Redeemer

Some of the psalms make predictions concerning the Messiah, Who would pay the redemption price for sin. Psalm 22 speaks of the Messiah's death. David wrote this psalm to describe his own experiences, but the Holy Spirit spoke through him to refer also to the Lord Jesus Christ.

The psalm begins with the words spoken by Jesus on the cross: "My God, my God, why hast thou forsaken me?" (22:1a; cf. Matt. 27:46). The psalm predicts the way that Israel would despise Jesus (Ps. 22:6, 7). The psalm provides the words spoken at Calvary by Jesus' religious opponents (22:8; also see Matthew 27:41–43). The psalm even predicts specific details of Jesus' crucifixion. People would gape at Him (Ps. 22:13, 17). They would pierce His hands and feet (22:16). His executioners would part His garments among them (22:18; cf. Matt. 27:35). And He would be thirsty (Ps. 22:15; cf. John 19:28). The psalm provides a truly remarkable set of predictions concerning the price that would be paid for redemption from sin.

17. As Christians we view the cross of Christ as both horrible and beautiful, how does this Psalm communicate both of these ideas?

18. How might we praise and thank God for our redemption?

Making It Personal

19. On another piece of paper, write a brief psalm expressing a personal response to God's greatness and to His grace in your life.

20. Why does writing your thoughts help you appreciate God?

21. Memorize Psalm 147:1.

Israel Practices God's Revelation and Redemption

God's revelation and redemption should result in holy, wise living.

Lev. 1—7; 11; 18; 21; 22; Job; Prov.; Eccles.

"Let us hear the conclusion of the whole matter: Fear God; and keep his commandments: for this is the whole duty of man" (Ecclesiastes 12:13).

Restaurants guard their recipes for their signature dishes so people can't order their dishes anywhere else. But smart cooks can figure out the recipes using trial and error, taste tests, and sometimes even chemistry. There are even websites that publish recipes that are very close to their restaurant counterparts.

Getting Started

1. What are the ingredients of your favorite recipe?

2. What "ingredients," or characteristics, are necessary for a godly life?

3. How would you rate the Old Testament as a recipe for godly living?

There are many different characteristics that are necessary for a godly life. However, two very important characteristics are holiness and wisdom. The Old Testament reveals much of the Christian understanding of these two important aspects to godly living.

Searching the Scriptures

Temple Traditions

4. Read Leviticus 19:2. According to this verse what is the basis for the need for human holiness?

5. How does the fact that the law reveals God's holiness make application by Christians easier?

God expected Israel to practice His self-revelation and redemption. The book of Leviticus outlines one of God's major expectations: "Ye shall be holy: for I the Lord your God am holy" (Lev. 19:2; cf. 11:44, 45; 20:7, 26). The book of Leviticus explains God's specific expectations regarding the priesthood, the sacrifices, the festivals, and the laws of ritual purity. God called Israel to respond to His revealed holiness by living holy lives. Israel became a separated and sanctified people when she followed the regulations of Leviticus.

When Israel left Egypt, God directed the nation to construct a portable temple, a tent-like structure called the tabernacle (Exod. 35—40). The Israelites relocated the tabernacle every time they journeyed in the wilderness. Many of the laws in Exodus and Leviticus explain God's regulations for the tabernacle rituals and eventually those of the temple. Other laws dealt with the daily life of each Israelite. The books of Leviticus and Exodus overlap in many of these concerns.

Devotion to God's Service

God required Israel's priests to be descendants of Moses' older brother, Aaron (Lev. 21:1). Moses and Aaron were Levites. The Levites assisted in the temple service, but only the descendants of Aaron could perform the sacrifices (Lev. 22:2; Exod. 2:1). Even then, only those descendants who were whole, unblemished, and unbroken could offer the sacrifices (Lev. 21:16–21).

The high priests wore special garments and submitted to even stricter standards. They could not defile themselves by coming near to a dead body, except for the closest of kin. And they could not participate in mourning rituals (21:1–5, 10, 11). Any daughter of a priest who profaned herself through immorality was to be burned with fire (22:9).

All of the requirements served to separate the priests and high to the service of the Lord.

6. What might you learn about the demands of God's holiness by considering the priesthood?

7. Read 1 Peter 1:15, 16; 2:5. How are Christians described in this passage?

8. How does God's expectations for the holiness of Old Testament priests compare to His expectations for the holiness of Christians?

The New Testament applies God's expectations of His Old Testament priests to the lives of New Testament believers (1 Pet. 1:15, 16; 2:5). Believers today, as a holy priesthood, offer up "spiritual sacrifices, acceptable to God." God expects us to live holy, separated lives.

Sacrifices: Obedience and Trust in God

The Lord directed Israel to offer only intact, unblemished animals (Lev. 22:17–33). The regulations concerning the unblemished priests and sacrifices prefigure the unblemished sacrifice of Jesus Christ (1 Pet. 1:19) and His perfect priesthood resulting in salvation for all who put their faith in Him (Heb. 5:1–10).

Some Bible scholars think that God forgave sins on the basis of sacrifices that were made in faith. Others think that the sacrifice merely righted the sinner's relationship within the theocracy. Both views have their merits. Since the sacrifices did not result in eternal life, nothing is said about faith in the Levitical directives. Salvation has always been by faith. A believing Israelite would obey the sacrificial system and trust that God would accept and forgive him. The sacrifices in this way were a precursor to the sacrifice of the promised Messiah. Yet the sacrifices could not in themselves remove sin. Only Jesus Christ could purge the sinful conscience; the blood of bulls and goats could never obtain "eternal redemption" (Heb. 9:11–14).

God expected all Israelites to offer sacrifices. At a minimum, they all were outwardly to submit to God's rule to fit within the theocracy. Not all who outwardly submitted, however, were forgiven sinners.

The Lord commanded the people of Israel to offer five major types of offerings. The initial regulations for these offerings appear in Leviticus 1:1—6:7. Additional requirements appear in 6:8—7:38.

Burnt offering (Lev. 1:3–17; 6:8–13). During the burnt offering, the repentant sinner watched as his unblemished male animal was sacrificed on the altar (Lev. 1:9). The entire animal, excluding the skin, was burned to signify dedication to God. The animal selection was based on the individual's wealth. The sinner identified the animal as his substitute. The animal's death atoned for his sins (1:4). This means the sin was covered in God's eyes.

9. Read Leviticus 1:9. Why would God find the smell of burning animals to be a sweet aroma?

Meat/grain offering (Lev. 2:1–16; 6:14–18). For the grain offering, the worshiper offered flour with oil and frankincense or baked grain or some of the first grain harvested (2:1, 2, 5, 14). The offering was a memorial probably in thanksgiving to God. All burnt offerings had accompanying grain offerings. The priests ate a portion of the grain offering (6:16–18). The absence of leaven in the offering pointed to the sinlessness of Christ.

Sin offering (Lev. 4:1—5:13; 6:24–30). Repentant Israelites who sinned unintentionally out of ignorance offered the sin offering (4:2, 13, 22, 27). It involved the sacrifice of a male or female sheep or goat and resulted in the atonement of the unwitting sin (4:35). The sin offering was a picture of Christ being made sin for sinners. The priests ate a portion of this offering (6:29).

Trespass/guilt offering (Lev. 5:14—6:7; 7:1–7). Israelites who sinned, especially against another Israelite, offered the trespass offering and made restitution to the person they wronged (6:1–5). The trespass offering involved the sacrifice of an unblemished ram (6:6). The priests ate a portion of this offering (7:6).

Peace/fellowship offering (Lev. 3:1–17; 7:11–21, 28–34). The Israelite who desired to renew his fellowship with God or to express his thanksgiving to God offered the peace offering. It entailed the sacrifice of an ox, sheep, or goat. Parts of the abdominal organs were burned (7:3–5). The worshiper ate other parts of the animal in a special fellowship meal between the person, his family, and God (7:15). The peace offering reminds us of the fellowship we enjoy with God and other believers by virtue of Christ's perfect sacrifice (Eph. 2:16).

10. What impressions would all these sacrifices and specific rules leave on the faithful Old Testament worshiper?

The word "unclean" appears more than one hundred times in Leviticus 11—15. These chapters outline God's specific requirements for holy living in the days of the theocracy. They cover diet, childbirth, and some diseases.

11. How would you define holiness?

12. In what areas of life should holiness exist?

Be Separate unto God

God expected Israel to eat only certain animals. In the beginning, all people were vegetarians, but after the Flood, God allowed people to eat meat. God revealed further dietary requirements in Leviticus 11. The Israelites could eat animals whose hoofs were parted all the way through and who also chewed the cud (Lev. 11:3–8). The legislation outlawed the eating of rabbits and pigs. The only fish allowed was that which had both fins and scales (11:9–12). The Lord specifically outlawed some twenty kinds of birds (11:13–19). He did allow the people to eat locusts and grasshoppers (11:20–23).

The primary reason why God banned the unclean animals was to prevent Israel from assimilating with the nations around her and to reinforce her separatism.

13. How would the identification of unclean animals also help Israel understand their place as God's chosen people?

Honor God's Way of Purity

Leviticus 18 spells out specific requirements related to sexual relations. God forbade incest (18:6–16). He did not permit a man to marry his wife's daughter, granddaughter, or sister (18:17, 18). He determined when it was appropriate for a husband and wife to have a physical relationship (18:19). He forbade adultery, fertility sacrifices, homosexuality, and bestiality (18:20–23). God repeatedly forbade all of these abominations. He promised to punish the pagan nations that practiced them by removing them from the Promised Land (18:24–30).

14. On what bases has society rewritten God's rules for sexuality?

The Holiness Laws, when followed, separated Israel unto God. Since God redeemed His people unto Himself, He expected them to respond with holiness in every area of their lives. The Old Testament story envisioned Israel as a holy nation with a holy priesthood. Unfortunately, Israel rarely obeyed God.

God not only expected holiness, He also expected wisdom. Wisdom is skill in living. Several books in the Old Testament emphasize the theme of wisdom. These books are Job, Proverbs, and Ecclesiastes.

15. Where might people go for wisdom today?

Job: Trust in God's Goodness and Power

We do know that Job was a historical person (James 5:11; Ezek. 14:14, 20). His longevity and wealth in livestock (42:12, 16) argue for a time simultaneous to the Patriarchs. The book treats the theological and philosophical topic called the problem of evil, or "theodicy" as it is technically called.

16. What are examples of questions people ask that indicate they are struggling with the existence of evil?

Job was a righteous man (Job 1:1), but he lost all his possessions and his children and his health (1:12—2:7). In spite of the terrible turn of events, Job did not "sin with his lips" (2:10). His three friends came to comfort Job (2:11), and the four of them discussed the nature of God and evil for most of the space of the book. Toward the end, a fourth friend, Elihu, spoke (32:1—37:24). Finally, God Himself spoke (38:1—42:6).

Job understood the nature of wisdom (28:28), but he had difficulty submitting to God's ways. Job defended his righteousness and demanded that God give him an explanation for all that had happened to him. Job also took heart in the promise of the resurrection (19:25, 26).

Job's three friends agreed among themselves that calamity befalls sinners. They saw God only in retributive terms.

Elihu came closest to the truth when he stated that God has other purposes for calamities besides punishment. Earlier, Job had agreed (23:10–12).

When God spoke, He did not answer Job. God never needs to defend His ways. He does whatever He wishes.

17. Read Job 38:4. What did God communicate to Job by asking him this question?

Job learned from God that people must simply trust in God's sovereignty. God disapproved of the speeches of the three friends (42:7). Given a Heavenly perspective (Job 1; 2), we learn that God does take note of the righteous and that their suffering is precious to Him.

We learn from Job that God's ways are far higher than our ways. We must trust His goodness and power even when life doesn't seem to make sense.

Proverbs: Accept God's Advice on Living

Solomon wrote many of the proverbs. A proverb is a short moralistic saying. It is an aphorism or a maxim that is typically true. A proverb is not a promise. The proverbs give guidance for godly living.

The first nine chapters are presented as parental advice to a young-adult son. Chapters 7 and 8 contrast the immoral woman with wisdom appearing as a woman. Chapters 10—23 provide numerous proverbs concerning the issues of daily life. Chapters 24—26 give advice on how to interact with various kinds of people (kings, enemies, fools, sluggards, and so forth). Chapters 27—29 impart wisdom for life and wealth. Chapter 30 teaches that the enemy of wisdom is pride. Chapter 31 appears in the form of an acrostic. It contains the famous description of the virtuous woman (31:10–31). The proverbs provide sage advice for all people of all times, but especially for believers. Those who fear the Lord will practice wisdom (1:7).

Ecclesiastes: Fear God and Keep His Commands

The third book of wisdom is Ecclesiastes. The book does not directly disclose its author, but he was a son of David (Eccles. 1:1), a man of unparalleled wisdom (1:16), and a man of unparalleled wealth (2:7). These descriptors point to King Solomon.

Ecclesiastes teaches how people can live a wise life even though we will never have all of the answers (3:11).

Three repeated themes punctuate the book and become important keys to unlocking the wisdom of this book. The first repeated theme is "vanity of vanities" (1:2). Seeking to find the ultimate answers to all of life questions from the buffet of life choices is a vain search. You will never find the answers to all of life questions.

The second repeated theme is the idea of eating, drinking, and enjoying life with the view that is a gift from God (2:24). Since no one could ever acquire all of the answers to life, we might as well enjoy the life God has given us, acknowledging God's ownership of everything.

Solomon describes the third theme as the end of the matter—fear God and keep His commandments (12:13). Not having all the answers is no excuse for living an ungodly life. Studying these three themes and their repetition through Ecclesiastes will not only help one understand the book but will provide skill in living.

Making It Personal

18. Rate yourself in the consistency of your general practice of holy, wise living as a testimony of God's self-revelation and His redemption. Write some bullet points related to areas for improvement, strengths to build upon, and areas for more investigation.

19. How could you increase your holiness and wisdom in life?

20. What specific choice will you make this week to be more holy and/or wise?

21. Memorize Ecclesiastes 12:13.

Israel Anticipates God's Ultimate Revelation and Redemption

God's ultimate revelation and redemption will occur in the future.

Jer. 31—33; Ezek. 37; Joel 1—3

"But this shall be the covenant that I will make with the house of Israel; After those days, saith the Lord, I will put my law in their inward parts, and write it in their hearts; and will be their God, and they shall be my people" (Jeremiah 31:33).

Nobody's perfect! Everyone knows that, but we still idolize people and deny they ever do anything wrong. At the same time, we have a hard time imagining ourselves being perfect. Yet that is what God will do one day for all those who have trusted in Christ for salvation. Living forever and never sinning is a mind-blowing thought!

Getting Started

1. Have you ever met someone who seemed to be perfect?

2. How much time passed before you saw he wasn't perfect?

This study will introduce the New Covenant, the final covenant of the Old Testament story. The New Covenant deals with the heart of mankind and further reveals the gracious and merciful nature of our God. The New Covenant makes a way for Israel to perfectly obey God in the future.

Searching the Scriptures

The Old Testament includes seventeen prophesy books. They extend from Isaiah through Malachi. Lamentations was written by the prophet Jeremiah to mourn the destruction of Jerusalem by the Babylonians. Isaiah, Jeremiah, Ezekiel, and Daniel are relatively large books. They are called the Major Prophets. The remaining twelve books, Hosea through Malachi, are called the Minor Prophets because of their relative brevity.

Prophets' Chronology

The seventeen prophetic books are grouped roughly by size and chronology. During the days of the divided monarchy, Hosea and Amos ministered to the Northern Kingdom of Israel. Isaiah, Jeremiah, Joel, Micah, Habakkuk, and Zephaniah ministered to the Southern Kingdom of Judah. Also during the divided monarchy, Obadiah spoke against Edom and Jonah and Nahum both spoke against Nineveh, Assyria's capital city.

Ezekiel and Daniel ministered during the years of exile in Babylon and Persia. Haggai, Zechariah, and Malachi ministered to the Jewish remnant that returned to the Promised Land.

Prophets' Major Themes

The prophets spoke as God's ordained spokesmen. They called people to repent of their sins, they warned people of impending judgment for sin, and they announced God's forgiveness to all who would repent. The prophets spoke to common people and to kings. They preached against Israelites and the heathen. They preached against the current sins of Israel, and they predicted future events. Their predictive ministry happened within the context of all these different ministry facets.

3. On what part of the prophets' ministry do you often focus?

4. What is the danger of only viewing the prophets' ministries as predicting the future?

When the prophets preached against sin, they found a moral basis for their sermons in the Sinaitic and Dueteronomic stipulations.

The prophets continually reminded the people to fulfill their covenant obligations. When the prophets made predictions concerning the future glory of Israel and the reign of the Messiah, they found a promissory basis in the Abrahamic and Davidic Covenants.

The prophets Isaiah, Jeremiah, and Ezekiel also spoke of a future New Covenant. The contrast between the various covenants manifests itself clearly in the prophets' prophetic sermons. Judgment would come because the conditional Sinaitic and Deuteronomic Covenants were broken. But God still had a plan for Israel because the unconditional Abrahamic and Davidic Covenants bound God to bless Israel ultimately.

5. How has learning about the covenants helped you understand God's dealings with Israel in the Old Testament?

The covenants provide the matrix for understanding God's relationship with Israel. They show not only why Israel remained God's chosen people but also why they suffered tremendous judgment for their sins.

The Day of the Lord

Many prophets referred to the distant future as the Day of the Lord. An Israelite day went from sundown to sundown. Therefore, opposite to the thinking of most of the modern world, a day in Israel began with the darkness of night and ended with light of day.

6. What expectations are created about the Day of the Lord as a time period when it is thought of as patterned after a Hebrew day?

At present, we are living in the Day of Man, a time when the Gentile nations and governments and courts hold judgment over the earth. At any moment, the Day of Jesus Christ will come to pass (Phil. 1:6). The Day of Jesus Christ is the rapture of the church. Then the world will enter the Day of the Lord with the darkness of the seven years of tribulation and the brightness of the millennial Kingdom. Finally, the Day of God will begin (1 Cor. 15:28) and continue without end for all eternity.

Darkness: Divine Judgment

During the days of the prophet Joel, a devastating locust plague came upon the land (Joel 1:1–3). The prophet saw the plague as divine judgment for breaking the Deuteronomic Covenant (Deut. 29:1–28).

7. Read Joel 1:4–7. How are the waves of attackers described?

8. According to verse 7, what is the extent of the damage done?

Joel invited the people to mourn like a betrothed virgin whose promised groom has died before the marriage could be consummated (1:8). Nothing remained to sacrifice as an offering to the Lord (1:9–13).

Joel used the occasion of the plague as an opportunity to describe the future Day of the Lord. Before it begins, Christ will return to the clouds to rapture His church unto Himself. With the church removed from the earth, the Lord will again deal with Israel according to the covenant stipulations. Consequently, Joel appealed to Israel of the future to repent. During the dark days of the Day of the Lord, catastrophe will follow catastrophe, and famine and hardship will plague the earth

(1:16–20). The time will be for "destruction from the Almighty" (1:15).

9. Read Joel 1:14–20. What would you conclude is God's desire in bringing about the darkness of the Day of the Lord?

During the dark days of the Day of the Lord, a mighty army will invade the Promised Land (Joel 2:2). The advancing army will slash and burn its way through Israel until the land is desolate (2:3).

Locusts are noisy, and their heads look somewhat like horses' heads. Joel used the similarities to describe the invading army with its horses, noisy chariots, and flaming destruction (2:4–6). Just as locusts climb walls and follow one after another, so also the invading army will scale fortifications and not break rank (2:7–9). Signs in the heavens will accompany the invasion (2:10, 11; Rev. 6:12, 13; 8:8–12). Joel then spoke to plead with Israelites who will face the Day of the Lord (Joel 2:12–17).

10. Read Joel 2:12, 13b. What does God ask Israel to do?

11. Read Joel 2:13–20. To what attributes of God did Joel point in his call for Israel's repentance?

Light: Divine Redemption

The Day of Lord will begin with divine judgment, but it will end with divine redemption and blessing. Israel will repent of her sins toward the end of the tribulation period; the people will listen to the voice of Joel. All Israel will be saved, and God will forgive their sins (Rom. 11:26, 27).

12. Read Joel 2:19–32. How is God's redemption of Israel characterized in these verses?

God will also take pity upon His people and be jealous for His land (Joel 2:18). He will destroy the northern army. The stench of their rotting corpses will fill the area between the Mediterranean and Dead Seas (2:20; cf. Ezek. 39:2). The Lord will restore the land's productivity (Joel 2:19, 22), and the rain will fall again (2:23). The people of Israel will have abundant harvests and have plenty to eat (2:24–26a). The nation as a whole will finally know the Lord for Who He is. They will praise Him for what He has done (2:26b, 27).

The Day of the Lord will include God's ultimate self-revelation and redemption. He personally will rescue Israel from her sins and her enemies. He personally will be "in the midst of Israel" (2:27).

Joel also predicted that God will pour out His Spirit upon all people (2:28, 29). The promise, when fulfilled, will be a fulfillment of Moses' desire (Num. 11:29). The outpouring will be accompanied by signs in the heavens (Joel 2:30, 31).

The timing of the Spirit outpouring is at the end of the Tribulation and beginning of the Millennium. At that time, whoever calls upon the Lord will be delivered (2:32). The deliverance will be both physical and spiritual. As the nation calls upon Jesus as Messiah, He will deliver the people from their enemies and sins and will give the people His Holy Spirit. And the land will be a place of deliverance instead of desolation (Zech. 12:10–14).

God will bring about a complete reversal in the fortunes of Israel and her enemies (Joel 3:1–21). God will defeat Israel's enemies in the valley of Jehoshaphat, also called the "valley of decision" (3:2, 12, 14). This valley, likely near to Jerusalem, was the site of the Lord's great victory in the days of King Jehoshaphat (2 Chron. 20:1–30). God will call the Gentiles to war to defeat them (Joel 3:9–13). (Compare the prophecy of verse 10 with the words of Isaiah 2:4 and Micah 4:3.) Signs will appear in the heavens (Joel 3:15; see again 2:30, 31). Then the Lord, Jesus Christ the Messiah, will dwell in Jerusalem (3:17; see again 2:27). A new river will flow from the temple mount eastward to the north end of the Dead Sea. The river will sweeten the waters of the Dead Sea (3:18; also see Ezekiel 47:1–12).

The New Covenant

13. Israel failed to keep the Sinaitic and Deuteronomic Covenants. If

God had given them even stricter laws to obey, would that have helped them be more obedient? Explain.

14. What did Israel need in order to obey God perfectly?

The Old Testament story of revelation and redemption begins with the Abrahamic Covenant and ends with the New Covenant. God revealed Himself to Abraham and promised Abraham that He would bless him and his descendants. Throughout the story of the Old Testament, however, Abraham's descendants disobeyed God. They chose to live outside the umbrella of God's blessings. The prophets faithfully warned the people and called them to repentance. Still, the nation for the most part lived in rebellion against God. In the end, the prophets looked forward to the future days when the Lord would change the heart of Israel.

The problem with the Sinaitic and Deuteronomic Covenants was their inability to enable Israel to obey. They merely provided an external impetus toward obedience with their threats of curses. Therefore, the Lord promised a New Covenant. The New Covenant promises an inward change in the heart of the people to enable them to obey (Jer. 31:32, 33; 32:39, 40). God's prophets told of the New Covenant.

15. Read Jeremiah 31:35–37. How does Jeremiah describe the unconditional nature of the New Covenant?

The New Covenant will be an unconditional covenant. The dependability of the movement of the sun, moon, and stars exemplifies the permanence of the New Covenant (Jer. 31:35, 36). The New Covenant will be an "everlasting covenant" (32:40; Ezek. 37:26).

The New Covenant promises an ultimate revelation of God and an ultimate national redemption. The Lord promised to put His Spirit upon His people and His words within them (Isa. 59:20, 21). God will put His law inside His people; He will write it upon their hearts. They and their descendents will be enabled to fear the Lord forever (Jer. 31:33a; 32:39).

Israel will enjoy fellowship with God (31:33b; 32:38). All the people of Israel will finally know the Lord (31:34a; Ezek. 16:61–63). God will forgive their iniquity (Jer. 31:34b). God will again gather His people from their dispersions and will settle them as a single nation in the Promised Land, never to be deported again (32:37; Ezek. 37:15–22).

God will rule His people in a perfect theocracy through the resurrected King David and under the supreme rule of Jesus Christ. The people will obey and dwell in the land forever (37:23–25). God will also establish His sanctuary among His people (37:26–28). Israel will rejoice in the deliverance from sin and from their enemies.

Making It Personal

Israel's history is fraught with disobedience and failure. But the promises of Israel's future tell a story of God's greatness.

16. What could you learn about God from the New Covenant?

17. How should you live knowing the Day of the Lord will end with the "daylight" of Christ's rule?

18. What will you do this week to live in light of eternity?

19. Memorize Jeremiah 31:33.

Concluding the Old Testament Story

The Old Testament story reveals God's work of redemption.

Deut. 6; 2 Chron. 34; 35; Ezek. 16; Zech. 14

"Thus saith the LORD; Cursed be the man that trusteth in man, and maketh flesh his arm, and whose heart departeth from the LORD. . . . Blessed is the man that trusteth in the LORD, and whose hope the LORD is" (Jeremiah 17:5, 7).

W e often become comfortable with our current perspectives and only see things in the manner we normally do. This study should have expanded your perspective on the Old Testament and its relevance. The Old Testament should now be more accessible and valuable to you.

Getting Started

1. How has your perspective of the Old Testament changed over this quarter of lessons?

2. What helpful connection have you made with your life of faith?

Searching the Scriptures

Exclusivist Monotheism

One of the major themes of the Old Testament story is monotheism, the belief in one God. The Old Testament assumes the existence of God. It begins with, "In the beginning God created" (Gen. 1:1). God is distinct from His creation. He is unique; He has no peers. The Old Testament does not teach atheism, pantheism, or polytheism.

Abraham's ancestors had been polytheists (Josh. 24:2). His grandson, Jacob, had polytheism in his family (Gen. 31:34; 35:2–4). Later Israel followed the false god Baal and misused the prophets (2 Chron. 36:15, 16). Nevertheless, the Old Testament unequivocally teaches exclusivist monotheism: God is the one and only God.

Only a fool would say, "There is no God" (Ps. 14:1). Atheism is foolish since "The fear of the Lord is the beginning of knowledge" (Prov. 1:7).

Exclusivist monotheism stands at the heart of the law of Moses. The first of the Ten Commandments reads, "Thou shalt have none other gods before me" (Exod. 20:3; Deut. 5:7). Israel's confession of faith, the *Shema* (Hebrew for "hear") teaches exclusivist monotheism (Deut. 6:4).

3. Read Deuteronomy 6:4. What is the clear message of this verse?

God, and no one else, deserves worship. He alone is God and "there is none else beside him" (Deut. 4:35, 39). He alone created the heavens and the earth (Isa. 45:18). He alone has existed from eternity past; He alone is perfect in justice and righteousness (45:21–23a). Every knee, therefore, should bow before Him (45:23b).

God demands complete worship; He will not share His glory. He demands total undivided love and loyalty (Deut. 6:5). He is a "jealous God," and expects His people to fear and serve Him alone (6:13–15). Little wonder that He told Israel to choose between Him and Baal (1 Kings 18:21).

But though God is unique, He is not aloof. He invites the humble of heart to enjoy close fellowship with Him (Isa. 57:15).

4. What does worship of other "gods" look like in American culture?

5. Do you think churches are in danger of losing (in practice) their commitment to monotheism? Explain.

6. What might be some warning signs of a Christian beginning to worship other "gods?"

Covenants

The covenants provide a table of contents for the Old Testament story. The story unfolds as each new covenant is revealed.

7. Why is it important to distinguish whether a covenant is conditional or unconditional?

God made an unconditional covenant with Abraham and his descendants and an unconditional covenant with David. God will make an unconditional covenant with all the people of Israel in the New Covenant.

The Sinaitic and Deuteronomic Covenants, on the other hand, promised conditional blessings and curses. When the Israelites broke the Sinaitic and Deuteronomic Covenants, the prophets threatened the people with covenant curses. Still, the prophets promised ultimate blessing, because they knew that God will faithfully honor the three unconditional covenants.

8. How would you describe Israel's level of faithfulness to her covenant commitments?

9. Read Ezekiel 16:15-34. How did God describe Israel's level of faithfulness?

10. How does this vivid portrait of Israel's unfaithfulness increase your appreciation for God's faithfulness?

In the beginning of her history, Israel was undesirable (Ezek. 16:3–5). Nevertheless, God pitied the nation by allowing it to exist and multiply in Egypt (16:6, 7). Then He entered into a covenant with the nation at Sinai (16:8). Similar to the way that a man marries his wife, God bound Himself to the nation. God cleaned and clothed and prospered the nation (16:9–14). However, Israel committed religious adultery by committing idolatry (16:15–22) and by forging alliances with other nations (16:23–34). Israel broke the conditional covenants of Sinai and Deuteronomy. Therefore, God promised to judge the nation.

God brought an invading army against His people. The army killed, burned, and carried out God's jealous anger and judgment (16:35–43). The Lord lamented the way that Israel behaved even worse than her religious relatives Sodom and Samaria (16:44–58). Since God chose to judge Sodom and Samaria, He would certainly judge Judah.

God promised to deal with Judah in the same way Judah had dealt with God—by breaking the conditional covenant of Sinai (16:59).

In the end, God would remember the unconditional Abrahamic Covenant He had made with Israel in the days of her youth (16:60). He would also establish a New Covenant (16:62) with the people so they would know Him and He would be pacified and no longer angry (16:62, 63).

Theocracy

11. Based on what you have learned about the Old Testament and Ancient Israel, how often did Israel function as a theocracy?

12. What prevented Israel from consistently being a theocracy?

The Old Testament tells the story of God's plan to establish His rule among His people. God's rule is known as the theocracy. The Old Testament clearly conveys the concept, but the people of Israel rarely practiced it. God wished to rule His people through His designated leaders, but Israel resisted (Hos. 8:4). God intended to exercise His will through submissive elders, judges, kings, priests, and prophets. God desired Israel to be a holy nation faithfully following His laws (Exod. 19:6–8).

The book of Deuteronomy functioned as the constitution for the theocracy. It provided the terms of agreement allowing Israel to live on the Promised Land under God's sovereign rule. The book of Deuteronomy provided legislation for the nation's kings (Deut. 17:14–20), prophets (18:13–19), and priests (31:9–13). In each of these cases, the legislation clearly stipulates that the human leader was to follow God's Word.

God directed the human king to write his own copy of the law. The king was supposed to keep his personal copy with him all the days of his life so he could learn to fear God and keep His statutes (Deut. 17:18, 19).

The prophet was supposed to speak God's words (18:18). Every seventh year during the Feast of Tabernacles, the priests were supposed to read the law aloud for all the people. All Israel was supposed to hear the law so that they would learn to fear the Lord and keep His Word (31:9–12). Each generation of Israelites needed to hear the Word of God (31:13).

During several key periods in Israel's history, the theocracy functioned properly. Most notably, several kings of Judah led the people to renew their covenant vows. The young king Josiah stands as one such exemplary leader in the theocracy.

13. Read 2 Chronicles 34:1, 8–33. Why was Josiah a good theocratic leader?

The Old Testament story looks forward to the ultimate theocracy when the Messiah will reign over His earthly kingdom. Passages such as Zechariah 14 vividly portray a future age when the Messiah will establish His rule over the earth. Right before the nations of the world overwhelm

Jerusalem, the Lord Jesus shall "go forth, and fight against those nations, as when he fought in the day of battle" (Zech. 14:3). He will set His feet upon the Mount of Olives, just east of the city of Jerusalem (14:4). He will make Jerusalem His capital city, "And the LORD shall be king over all the earth: in that day shall there be one LORD, and his name one" (14:9).

Redemption

The Old Testament tells the history of God's work of redemption. Since Adam and Eve sinned, all their descendents have been under the curse of sin. God, however, has worked from before the creation of the world to redeem sinful humanity (Eph. 1:4). God is the redeemer (Isa. 41:14; 44:6).

After Adam and Eve fell into sin, death reigned. People devoted themselves to do evil. God judged the world with the Flood, but He rescued Noah and his family. People again populated the earth. God chose Abraham from among the nations so that in him and in his descendents "all families of the earth" might be blessed (Gen. 12:3; Deut. 14:2; Ps. 135:6).

God redeemed the Israelites from slavery in Egypt and brought them safely through the Red Sea (Exod. 6:6). Then the Lord gave Israel His law.

The law was a priceless gift. It listed God's exact expectations and showed the people how short they fell from God's holy standard (Ps. 19:7; Rom. 3:20). The law indicated the need for a Substitute Who would take the punishment for sin. The Old Testament sacrificial system pointed forward to the ultimate sacrifice of Christ (Isa. 52:13—53:12; Heb. 4:14, 15).

Since the law proved the sinfulness of all, it also proved that there is nothing good that a person can do to earn favor from God. Instead, the repentant sinner needs to simply trust in God—to take Him at His Word (Jer. 17:5-7; Heb. 11:39).

14. Read Leviticus 25:25-28, 47-55. What did the people do when they redeemed land or slaves?

15. How does this redemptive action compare to your salvation?

The Old Testament law allowed the Israelites to buy back land that they had sold. They could pay the price to redeem it. Slaves could be set free if relatives paid their redemption price (Lev. 25:25–28, 47–55). These laws afford a beautiful picture of redemption. Someone must pay the price.

When it comes to sin, no mere human being can pay the price. Just as God redeemed His people from their Babylonian captivity (Jer. 50:33, 34), so He can redeem sinful humanity. God did this by sending His Son so He might die as the sinless Man for all of humanity. Christ died to assuage God's righteous wrath toward sinful humanity. The Old Testament gives the early history of God's work toward redemption. The New Testament is the sequel. It shows how God's work was finished (John 19:30).

Connections between the Testaments

The Old Testament looks forward to the New Testament with its types. A type is a person, event, or object in the Old Testament that finds correspondence in the New Testament. Technically, the New Testament must declare that such a correspondence exists. Moses' bronze serpent is a type (Num. 21:5–9).

16. Read Numbers 21:5–9; John 3:14, 15. How does the account of Moses' bronze serpent prefigure the work of Christ on the cross?

One of the most obvious connections between the two Testaments manifests itself in the 295 clear references to the Old Testament that appear in the New Testament. In fact, 353 verses in the New Testament are quotations that come from the Old Testament. The Old Testament provided Jesus and His apostles with texts for their preaching, teaching, and writing.

The Old Testament joins the New Testament with the connection of predictions and fulfillments. The Old Testament contains numerous predictions, and the New Testament contains numerous fulfillments. This phenomenon argues for the divine origin of the Old Testament.

Many of the predictions in the Old Testament are messianic. They find their fulfillment in Jesus Christ. Therefore, the promises of God in the

Old Testament find the "yea" in Jesus Christ. As New Testament believers, we say "Amen" to this Christological fulfillment (2 Cor. 1:20).

Looking beyond their near history, the prophets looked forward to a distant future, to an ultimate period of revelation and redemption. These prophecies center in the suffering and reign of King David's Great Descendant. The Jewish people in Jesus' day were confused about these disparate kinds of prophecies. How could the Messiah both suffer and reign? During His earthly ministry, Jesus Christ provided the solution. The Old Testament teaches that Christ (Messiah) must suffer and rise from the dead (Isa. 53; Luke 24:46). Jesus fulfilled all the prophecies about His suffering. But what about all the other prophecies about Messiah's glorious reign? Jesus Christ promised that He would return one day to the earth and fulfill all these other prophecies (Luke 22:16, 18, 30).

Making It Personal

17. Which of God's characteristics do you appreciate more after studying the Old Testament this quarter?

18. Which account or lesson helped heighten this appreciation?

19. How are you better equipped to use the Old Testament to encourage others?

20. Complete the following phrase: "I praise God for the Old Testament because . . ."

21. Memorize Jeremiah 17:5 and 7.